A Terence Reader

ℬℭ LATIN Readers

Series Editor:
Ronnie Ancona

These readers, written by experts in the field, provide well annotated Latin selections to be used as authoritative introductions to Latin authors, genres, or topics, for intermediate or advanced college Latin study. Their relatively small size (covering 500–600 lines) makes them ideal to use in combination. Each volume includes a comprehensive introduction, bibliography for further reading, Latin text with notes at the back, and complete vocabulary. Nineteen volumes are scheduled for publication; others are under consideration. Check our website for updates: www.BOLCHAZY.com.

A Terence Reader
Selections from Six Plays

William S. Anderson

Bolchazy-Carducci Publishers, Inc.
Mundelein, Illinois USA

Series Editor: Ronnie Ancona
Volume Editor: Laurie Haight Keenan
Cover Design & Typography: Adam Phillip Velez

A Terence Reader
Selections from Six Plays

William S. Anderson

© 2009 Bolchazy-Carducci Publishers, Inc.
All rights reserved.

Bolchazy-Carducci Publishers, Inc.
1570 Baskin Road
Mundelein, Illinois 60060
www.bolchazy.com

Printed in the United States of America
2009
by United Graphics

ISBN 978-0-86516-678-3

Library of Congress Cataloging-in-Publication Data

Terence.
  [Selections. English & Latin. 2009]
 A Terence reader : selections from six plays / William S. Anderson.
    p. cm. -- (Latin readers)
 Includes bibliographical references and index.
 ISBN 978-0-86516-678-3 (pbk. : alk. paper) 1. Terence--Translations into English. 2.
Latin drama (Comedy)--Translations into English. 3. Latin language--Readers. I. Anderson,
William Scovil, 1927- II. Title.
 PA6756.A1A53 2009
 872'.01--dc22

2009019841

Contents

Preface vii

Introduction ix

Latin Text, Six Plays 1
   Andria, 28–139 1
   Heauton, 175–256 5
   Phormio, 1–12, 884–989 9
   Hecyra, 198–28 14
   Eunuchus, 539–614 17
   Adelphoe, 1–25, 787–881 21

Commentary 27
   Andria, Starting the Plot, 28–139 27
   Heauton, Complications, 175–256 35
   Phormio, Plot Summary
      and Vigorous Ending, 1–12, 884–989 41
   Hecyra, Misunderstandings, 198–280 51
   Eunuchus, Characterization, 539–614 56
   Adelphoe, Prologue and Ending, 1–25, 787–88 65

Appendix: Comic Meters in Terence 77

Vocabulary 81

Preface

It is a considerable relief to have completed this study of Terentian comedy and a particular pleasure to be giving some credit to those who have helped to bring things to this comfortable (at last) stage. When Terence completed his plays, he readied them for performance by composing a preface (or Prologus) to establish initial contact with the audience. He found himself in a special situation as he addressed the audience about particular features of his inspiration and purposes in his new drama. But he did not voice his pleasure with his creative process, nor did he stress the satisfaction with having completed his poetic task. Instead of thanking those, if there were any, who helped him finish a play, he regularly assailed the incredible negligence with which his critics operated. It is difficult to imagine Terence using the comic mask as he hectored his rival Luscius or the "stupidity" of the Roman populace for walking out on a previous comedy and halting its presentation.

I have been more fortunate than Terence in my first efforts to prepare this book, and a smile, not a frown registers itself on my face as I write these words. I have of course experienced some criticism, but unlike that which victimized Terence, it was not aimed to destroy my ego or to drive the comedy off the stage. My useful critics combined their efforts to rescue Terence from my over-enthusiasm. He, too, would have been grateful for such creative and knowledgeable critics working with him. My principal advisers, whom I wish especially to thank, were a team of two, the editor for the series, Ronnie Ancona, who frequently and correctly called me to account on my interpretations of the Latin text of Terence, and Laurie H. Keenan, who represented the interests and concerns of the printer and the technical effort to realize in print what had been proposed by the Latinists. She arranged with Oxford University Press for my use of the relevant pages of the Oxford Classical Text of Terence, edited by Lindsay and Kauer and reprinted in 1979. I have followed the OCT in all matters except in the representation of incomplete or interrupted speech, where I used the American convention of three dots instead of the OCT two.

I would like to thank for careful reading of a near-final stage of my manuscript two astute and anonymous readers. Tom Harrington formulated swiftly and skillfully a full and useful Vocabulary.

And finally I would like to profess my gratitude to my wife Deirdre, who helped me with her friendly support through this long process and through her mastery of the computer when, as often, the machine threatened to halt my progress.

Kensington, California
March 30, 2009

Introduction

ᐸᴥ *Comedy before Terence*

Roman literature, it is often said, began with the presentation of one or two plays in 240 BCE at the festival that celebrated victory over the Carthaginians and the ending of the First Punic War. If comedies, they were received with such delight, that they were the beginning of more than a century of pleasure for the Roman people. Of all the comedies that were annually performed and all the other literary writings of that period, there have survived twenty plays of Plautus and six of Terence, all comedies and no other complete works but a prose treatise of Cato. We focus on Terence in this book.

Those first dramas in 240 were Greek plays in Latin, written by Livius Andronicus, a Greek from Southern Italy, Tarentum, who knew Latin well enough, but had little interest in producing an example of Roman culture. His actors were probably Greek slaves; they followed a plot that was laid in Athens and its vicinity; and they dressed like Greeks and pretended to be Greeks who had never heard of Rome. Roman comedy developed as drama in Greek dress with plots adapted for a Roman audience, that is, in Latin, but otherwise ostensibly Greek. Because the daily dress of a Greek was a cloak called *pallium*, the comedies of Plautus (250–180 BCE) and Terence (about 200–160 BCE) in Greek dress were called *palliatae*.

There were several distinct effects to be found in these *palliatae*. On the one hand, entering into this unusual dramatic world of Greek characters was escapist: it turned the audience on festival occasions away from their daily life as hard working and fighting Romans and encouraged them to relax with the normally trivial, even silly problems of these Greeks. But not everybody admired Greeks in the third and second centuries. So in contrast to this lazy temporary escapism, was the sense of superiority that many Romans, including the playwrights like Plautus, felt toward the somewhat decadent and impolitic civilization of Greece. After all, the Romans had been defeating and conquering the Greeks and they had looted Greece's treasures, works of art, and its libraries. For many Romans, then, the Greek civilization of the past conflicted with the corruption of the present and stimulated a feeling of ambiguity. Nevertheless, the artistic polish of these Latin Greek comedies could not be denied, and later poets learned much from them that they would never care to abandon.

One way of doing comedy, which we see often in contemporary TV comedies, is to make the characters and their plot ridiculous. The actors overact and over-emote and force us to laugh at them, not with them. The obvious jokes that could be made on Greek being staged in Latin were very popular. Changed emphasis on standard characters allowed down-playing the family situations of the original Greek play and a new stress on the clever and impudent slave who shapes the situation to his wishes and becomes the "hero." These are some of the special qualities of Plautus' plays before Terence.

∽ Terence's Comedy

Another way of doing Greek comedy was to take the plots, Greek though they were, and treat them with a certain amount of respect as real human situations, about which people of any culture could form intelligent opinions. It was less important that they were dressed like Greeks and walking the streets of an imaginary Athens than that they were human beings not too far different from us (if sympathetically staged). This seems to have been the inspiration of Terence. Instead of mocking the plots he used as hackneyed, he enriched them by dramatizing them as situations that did not necessarily end with everyone living happily ever after, by raising questions about dominant fathers and disobedient sons. He found escape from Rome and its political rivalries by following his Greek sources and practically ignoring the wars that raged in his time and had raged in the period of the Greek originals. A young man in Terence's comedies did not look forward to a political career and victorious wars abroad against foreign enemies. Instead, his future depended on how he played his role in family relationships, how he married, and what he could contribute to the future prosperity of his small clan.

Terence himself was not Roman by birth, not even Italian, and he grew up as an outsider to the Roman ideals as well as to the moral values of the *palliatae*, which he probably first came to know in his youth in Rome. On his origin and birth, there is permanent disagreement, it seems. The information that Suetonius collected has little authority, but many of his sources agree that Terence was born a slave, served in the household of Terentius Lucanus (otherwise unknown), and was freed by his generous master at an early age. If we try to put dates on these tenuous facts, we cannot accept the information that he was of the same age as Scipio Aemilianus (born 184)—that would make him eighteen at the time of his first comedy, *Andria*, in 166— nor can we guess how he became an African slave (in Carthage?) and then came to Rome nearly twenty years after hostilities in Africa with the Carthaginians had temporarily ended and the excuse was lost for the enslavement of this nameless child who became Terence because of his Roman master. It is tempting to speculate on Terence's sense of not belonging to Rome, but that is only speculation. He does not make that an issue of his comedies.

It must have taken Terence a good many years to perfect his Latin and to become master of the genre of comedy and theatrical practices. No information about his training in comedy survives, and he seems to burst on the scene in 166, when his first play, the *Andria*, was staged. It was a success, we may assume, because Terence immediately set to work on a second comedy for the following year, to be called *Hecyra* or *Mother-in-Law*. Staging it proved a disappointment for the poet and the troupe of actors: before the comedy had advanced very far, the lively circus atmosphere of the Roman holiday attracted his initial audience out of the theatre to the acrobatics of a tightrope walker, and the performance was aborted. This made Terence very bitter, for he was convinced of the merits of his play (which I, too, think is an excellent play, needing no excuses).

He came back in 163 with still another good comedy, *Heautonti-moroumenos* or *Self-Tormentor*, with two plays in 161, first *Eunuch*, an audience favorite, followed later in the year by *Phormio*, and finally he staged *Brothers* in 160. After that productive period, Terence and his comedies mysteriously disappeared. His ending is as mysterious as his beginning, and later Romans knew no more of him than we do today.

The comedies were commissioned by the Roman officials called aediles, and they arranged with a dramatic producer to stage the plays at official expense, free for the Roman populace. Most of Terence's plays were performed on the holiday in early April dedicated to the Great Mother (*Ludi Megalenses*). An alternative occasion was the holiday of the Roman Games in September. Some Roman families honored a dead hero of their clan by giving funeral games to attract the public, and on the death of Aemilius Paulus in early 160, his family had such games, including comedies, as part of the entertainment. This was the occasion for the presentation of *Brothers* and also for a second, similarly failed staging of the ill-fated *Hecyra*.

There are two purposes of this book: (1) To give students an introduction to the art of Terence as a comic poet; (2) To gain familiarity with and appreciation for the Latin of Terence. So far, we have briefly discussed the development of Roman comedy and the life of Terence. It is appropriate, then, to continue with the consideration of Terence as a comic poet. Four of his six plays were adapted from originals by Menander (342–291), the subtlest of the Greek comic dramatists who flourished at the end of the fourth century. The other two, *Hecyra* and *Phormio*, came from a younger admirer of Menander by the name of Apollodoros. In an arbitrary way, we can divide the plays into a beginning, a middle, and an end. In the beginning, the poet gives us some necessary background to the plot and the main characters. There is trouble for some people, but they cannot figure out how to deal with it. In some cases, the characters cannot even define their trouble within limits. Menander and the other Greeks seem to have used a divine narrator early in the play to give the audience privileged information; Terence interfered with this divine narrator and preferred that the audience remain as ignorant as the characters until the right time for both. Thus, he emphasizes a favorite theme of comedy: that characters are painfully trying to discover who they are, and the pursuit of knowledge is more serious than humorous. His audiences have no ironic advantage over the ignorant actors, so that the prevailing anxieties of the comedy affect the audience, too, until the final discovery or solution of ignorance enables them to achieve some security and happiness.

The problems of the play are not overtly political or of public significance: they affect one or two families at most, families of a father, a son, and sometimes a daughter, whose principal concern in life is arranging a suitable marriage for the son and heir. It may be that the problem originated years ago, when the daughter was born. More often in the plays we possess, the girl is the beloved of a neighbor son, and the two have managed to get the girl pregnant by careless passion; alternatively, the pregnancy resulted from rape. In any case, the pregnancy is a challenge of the father's authority and a threat to family unity, and the son does his best to conceal it from his father's wrath. Complications develop in the middle of the play, as the father discovers what the son is trying to conceal, that a socially forbidden love has arisen and now the girl is pregnant or her baby is actually born (*Andria* or *Adelphoe*). A surprise pregnancy confounds *Hecyra*, and a sudden birth greets the young man on his return from a trip. The ending of the play provides the final discoveries that permit the family to settle their difficulties. Menander, by contrast, seems to have made these settlements a lot simpler than Terence does. Sometimes, the father is so angry that he refuses to be appeased when everything can now be solved. Sometimes, in fact, as in *Phormio*, the father has something he needs to conceal from his wife, and it is the low-class parasite who ironically saves the family. (The parasite in Greco-Roman comedy is a character who by flattery and services earns his dinner.) And in the most ingenious and trenchant rejection of the "happy ending," in *Hecyra*, the young man tries to block the details of his rape from being known by his elders.

Thus, the plays of Terence emphasize the questions and uncertainties of the characters as they try to conceal what they have done (fallen in love, raped a girl) and they enact their search and discovery of who they are, what kind of son or man each is, and they implicitly become more mature members of the family as the result of their anxieties. He likes to show up the human errors of people, as for instance the snobbish ways of the older men, who think they are superior to a parasite because they have more money than he does (money that has been stolen from the estate of a wife). Or he shows older husbands roaring out their anti-feminist prejudices when they generalize (incorrectly in this instance of *Hecyra*) about the way mothers-in-law menace the happiness of their daughters-in-law. By leaving some of the problems unsettled, Terence complicates the proverbial "happy endings" of his predecessors or the original Greek play and closes with something like grim irony rather than general thanksgiving.

∾ The Latin in Terence's Comedies

Now, let us look at the Latin that Terence writes. We don't know at what age the African boy entered the household in Rome as slave of Terentius Lucanus. If he arrived as a baby, then Latin was his first language, and he knew no foreign first tongue. He certainly displays the mastery of Latin that made him a school teacher to later Romans, still respected and used in the fourth century CE. At some later age, after conquering Latin, Terence then proceeded to learn Greek, so that he could handle the original poets of the comedies that he would be producing in Rome. Aemilius Paullus had impounded the library of Perseus after defeating him and his Macedonians at Pydna at 168, and this library was available to the Roman reader with its rich Greek volumes. There, Terence may have read his first Menander. And it was to further his knowledge of Menander, to locate plays missing from the Roman library, that Terence intended, it seems, to travel to Greece after 160, but died in that laudable pursuit. The general nature of Menandrian Greek is simplicity and clarity, not artificial and stagy eloquence. Terence's Latin strikes us with similar virtues.

∾ Orthography and Grammar

Latin in the second century BCE had reached a stage of development where the pronunciation and spelling of certain words was what we now call "late archaic." For example, interconsonantal short *u* had

not yet become short *i*, as it would during the next century. I refer to such words as *facillume, lubidinem*, and *lacrumae* where each
short *u* became the short *i* you learned in your beginning Latin (the
Latin of Cicero in the first century). Those forms may be found in
Andria 65, 78, and 126. The second syllable of *advorsum* (found in
Andria 42) was already unstable in Terence's Latin. Thus, we find
the participle *adversus* in 64. Again, pronunciation of the two forms
yields similar sounds and makes the unfamiliar archaic word easy
to recognize. Interrogative "why" regularly appears as *quor*, soon to
become what you know as *cur*. (Cf. *Andria* 47, 103, 134.) It seems likely that Terence used alternative forms (e.g., *siem, sies, siet*, and the
old spelling of passive infinitives) for metrical convenience. Terence
uses the preposition *cum*, but the conjunction *quom*. The declen-
sion of the relative pronoun *qui* proceeds with a genitive *quoius* and
dative *quoi* (*Heauton* 233–34), but dative *cui* (*Andria* 167) indicates
that two forms were contemporary for Terence. The word for "son"
might surprise you as *gnatus*, but it will soon become *natus*. Finally,
in this short list of archaic forms, I mention that verbs compounded
with a preposition did not in Terence assimilate the final consonant
of the preposition, as they did regularly in Cicero's day. Hence, our
text gives us *inportunus*, not *imp-*, *inpeditae*, not *imp-*, *ecfertur*, not
eff-, and *conlocarunt*, not *coll-*. The dictionary provided in this book
spells the words in the pre-assimilated form used by Terence, which
should ease any difficulty.

Finally, a few remarks about Latin grammar in Terence. I said
at the start that he aimed at and succeeded in imitating the smooth
easiness of Menander, his favorite Greek source. Both in substantial
speeches and in the quick responses of animated conversation, Terence achieves simplicity and clarity. There are times when he produces a modest rhetorical wit, which for the most part is his own
creation. For example, in *Andria* 43–44, a character says: *nam istaec
commemoratio / quasi exprobratiost inmemoris benefici* ("That re-
minder of yours is like a reproach against one forgetful of a kindness").
There is no difficulty in the Latin grammar, but Terence has worked
hard to achieve this almost proverbial clarity. In doing so, he has
been the first user of the long nouns *exprobatio* and *commemoratio*,

which no one will use again until Cicero. Notice, too, the use of *in-memoris*, to allude to the first noun. The slave in *Andria* 218 in a single line dismisses the rash ways of lovers: *nam inceptiost amentium, haud amantium* ("That is an enterprise typical of madmen, not lovers.") The wit is that of Terence's actor: it could not have been translated from Menander's Greek, because Greek does not have a verbal pun like this on love and madness. Terence sought to give the impression of colloquial Latin among well-schooled men and women, for an audience that he preferred to be well schooled. His sharpest criticism of the Roman audience is voiced at the "stupid people" (*populus stupidus*) who ruined the first performance of *Hecyra* by rushing off to watch an acrobat rather than listen to his Latin. Compensation of a sort came to him, when he became a school author for Roman students and now, I hope, for you.

ᐩ *Suggested Reading*

Anderson, William S. 2000. "The Frustration of Anagnorisis in Terence's *Hecyra*." In *Essays in Honor of Katherine Geffcken*. Bolchazy-Carducci. 311–23.

———. 2001. *The Problem of Humor for an Ex-Slave*. Gail A. Burnett Lecture in Classics. San Diego.

———. 2002. "Resistance to Recognition and 'Privileged Recognition' in Terence." *CJ* 98:1–8.

———. 2004. "The Invention of Sosia for Terence's First Comedy: The *Andria*." *Ramus* 33. 1–2:1–9.

Arnott, W. G. 1970. "*Phormio parasitus*: a Study in Dramatic Methods of Characterization." *Greece & Rome* 17:32–57.

Barsby, J. A. 1993. "Problems of Adaptation in the *Eunuchus* of Terence." *Beitraege zum Antiken Drama und seiner Rezeption*. Stuttgart. 168–79.

Brothers, A. J. 1980. "The Construction of Terence's *Heautontimoroumenos*." *Classical Quarterly* 74: 94–117.

Dessen, C. S. 1993. "The Figure of the Eunuch in Terence's *Eunuchus*." *Helios* 22: 123–37.

Fantham, E. 1971. "*Heautontimoroumenos* and *Adelphi*: A Study of Fatherhood in Terence and Menander." *Latomus* 30: 970–98.

Fitzgerald, W. 2000. Slavery *and the Roman Literary Imagination*. Cambridge.

Gilula, D. 1980. "The Concept of the *bona meretrix*. A Study of Terence's Courtesans." *Rivista di Filologia* 108: 142–65.

Goldberg, S. M. 1986. *Understanding Terence*. Princeton.

Johnson, W. R. 1968. "Micio and the Perils of Perfection." *California Studies in Classical Antiquity* 1:171–86.

Konstan, D. 1983. *Roman Comedy*. Ithaca.

McCarthy, K. 2000. *Slaves, Masters, and the Art of Authority in Plautine Comedy*. Princeton.

———. 2004. "The Joker in the Pack: Slaves in Terence." *Ramus* 33.1–2: 100–19.

McGarrity, T. 1978. "Thematic Unity in Terence's *Andria*." *TAPA* 108: 103–14.

Moore, T. J. 1998. *The Theater of Plautus: Playing to the Audience*. Austin, TX.

———. 1999. "Facing the Muse: Character and Musical Accompaniment in Roman Comedy." *Syllecta Classica* 10: 130–53.

———. 2001. "Who is the Parasite? Giving and Taking in *Phormio*." In *Greek and Roman Comedy: Translations and Interpretations of Four Representative Plays*. Edited by Shawn O'Bryhim. Austin, TX: 254–65.

———. 2008. "When Did the *Tibicen* Play? Meter and Musical Accompaniment in Roman Comedy." *TAPA* 138: 3–46.

Richardson, L. 1997. "The Moral Problems of Terence's *Andria* and Reconstruction of Menander's *Andria* and *Perinthia*." *Greek, Roman and Byzantine Studies* 38:173–85.

Smith, L. P. 1994. "Audience Response to Rape: Chaerea in Terence's *Eunuchus*." *Helios* 21: 21–38.

Latin Text

∾ *1. ANDRIA 28–139*

SIMO   SOSIA

SI. Vos istaec intro auferte: abite.—Sosia,

ades dum: paucis te volo. *SO.* dictum puta:

30 nempe ut curentur recte haec? *SI.* immo aliud. *SO.* quid est

quod tibi mea ars efficere hoc possit amplius?

SI. nil istac opus est arte ad hanc rem quam paro,

sed eis quas semper in te intellexi sitas,

fide et taciturnitate. *SO.* exspecto quid velis.

35 *SI.* ego postquam te emi, a parvolo ut semper tibi

apud me iusta et clemens fuerit servitus

scis. feci ex servo ut esses libertus mihi,

propterea quod servibas liberaliter:

quod habui summum pretium persolvi tibi.

40 *SO.* in memoria habeo. *SI.* haud muto factum. *SO.* gaudeo

si tibi quid feci aut facio quod placeat, Simo,

et ĭd gratum fŭisse advorsum te habeo gratiam.

sed hŏc mihi molestumst; nam istaec commemoratio

quasi exprobratiost inmemoris benefici.

45 quin tu uno verbo dic quid est quod me velis.

SI. ita faciam. hoc primum in hac re praedico tibi:

quas credis esse has non sunt verae nuptiae.

SO. quor simulas igitur? *SI.* rem omnem a principio audies:

1

êo pacto et gnati vitam et consilium meum

50   cognosces et quid facere in hac re te velim.

nam is postquam excessit ex ephebis, Sosia, <et>

† liberius vivendi fuit potestas † (nam antea

qui scire posses aut ingenium noscere,

dum aetas metus magister prohibebant? *SO.* itast.)

55   *SI.* quod plerique omnes faciunt adulescentuli,

ut animum ad aliquod studium adiungant, aut equos

alere aut canes ad venandum aut ad philosophos,

horum ille nil egregie praeter cetera

studebat et tamen omnia haec mediocriter.

60   gaudebam. *SO.* non iniuria; nam id arbitror

adprime in vita esse utile, ut nequid nimis.

SI. sic vita erat: facile omnis perferre ac pati;

cum quibus erat quomque una îs sese dedere,

êorum obsequi studiis, adversus nemini,

65   numquam praeponens se illis; ita ŭt facillume

sine ïnvidia laudem invenias et amicos pares.

SO. sapienter vitam instituit; namque hoc tempore

obsequium amicos, veritas odium parit.

SI. interea mulier quaedam abhinc triennium

70   ex Andro commigravit huc viciniae,

inopia et cognatorum neglegentia

coacta, egregia forma atque aetate integra.

SO. ei, vereor nequid Andria adportet mali!

SI. primo haec pudice vitam parce ac duriter

75   agebat, lana ac tela victum quaeritans;

sed postquam amans accessit pretium pollicens

unus et item alter, ita ut ingeniumst omnium
hominum ab labore proclive ad lubidinem,
accepit condicionem, de(h)inc quaestum occipit.
80 qui tum illam amabant forte, ita ut fit, filium
perduxere illuc, secum ut una esset, meum.
egomet continuo mecum "certe captus est:
habet." observabam mane illorum servolos
venientis aut abeuntis: rogitabam "heus puer,
85 dic sodes, quis heri Chrysidem habuit?" nam Andriae
illi id erat nomen. *SO.* teneo. *SI.* Phaedrum aut Cliniam
dicebant aut Niceratum; †nam î tres tum simul†
amabant. "eho quid Pamphilus?" "quid? symbolam
dedit, cenavit." gaudebam. item alio die
90 quaerebam: comperibam nil ad Pamphilum
quicquam attinere. enĭmvero spectatum satis
putabam et magnum exemplum continentiae;
nam qui cum ingeniis conflictatur ei(u)s modi
neque commovetur animus in ea re tamen,
95 sciăs posse habere iam ipsum suâe vitae modum.
quom id mihi placebat tum uno ore omnes omnia
bona dicere et laudare fortunas meas,
qui gnatum haberem tali ingenio praeditum.
quid verbis opus est? hac fama inpulsus Chremes
100 ultro ad me venit, unicam gnatam suam
cum dote summa filio uxorem ut daret.
placuit: despondi. hic nuptiis dictust dies.
SO. quid obstat quor non verae fiant? *SI.* audies.
ferme in diebu' paucis quibus haec acta sunt

105 Chrysis vicina haec moritur. *SO.* o factum bene!
    beasti; eî metui a Chryside. *SI.* ibi tum filius
    cum illis qui amabant Chrysidem una aderat frequens;
    curabat una funu'; tristis interim,
    nonnumquam conlacrumabat. placuit tum id mihi.

110 sic cogitabam "hic parvae consuetudinis
    causa huiu' mortem tam fert familiariter:
    quid si ipse amasset? quid hîc mihi faciet patri?"
    haec ego putabam esse omnia humani ingeni
    mansuetique animi officia. quid multis moror?

115 egomet quoque eiu' causa in funus prodeo,
    nil suspicans etiam mali. *SO.* hem quid id est? *SI.* scies.
    ecfertur; imus. interea inter mulieres
    quae ibi aderant forte unam aspicio adulescentulam
    forma . . . *SO.* bona fortasse. *SI.* et voltu, Sosia,

120 adeo modesto, adeo venusto ut nil supra.
    quia tum mihi lamentari praeter ceteras
    visast et quia erat forma praeter ceteras
    honesta ac liberali, accedo ad pedisequas,
    quae sit rogo: sororem esse aiunt Chrysidis.

125 percussit ilico animum. attat hoc illud est,
    hinc illae lacrumae, haec illast misericordia.
    SO. quam timeo quorsum evadas! *SI.* funus interim
    procedit: sequimur; ad sepulcrum venimus;
    in ignem inpositast; fletur. interea haec soror

130 quam dixi ad flammam accessit inprudentius,
    sati' cum periclo. ibi tum exanimatus Pamphilus
    bene dissimulatum amorem et celatum indicat:

adcurrit; mediam mulierem complectitur:

"mea Glycerium," inquit "quid agis? quor te is perditum?"

135 tum illa, ut consuetum facile amorem cerneres,

reiecit se in eum flens quam familiariter!

SO. quid ais? *SI.* redeo inde iratus atque aegre ferens;

nec satis ad obiurgandum causae. diceret

"quid feci? quid commerui aut peccavi, pater?"

⁂ *2. HEAUTON 175–256*

CLITIPHO   CHREMES

175 *CL.* Nil adhuc est quod vereare, Clinia: haudquaquam etiam cessant

et ĭllam simŭl cum nuntio tibi hĭc adfuturam hodie scio.

proin tu sollicitudinem istam falsam quae te excruciat mittas.

   CH. quicum loquitur filius?

CL. pater adest quem volui: adibo. pater, opportune advenis.

180 *CH.* quid id est? *CL.* hunc Menedemum nostin nostrum vicinum? *CH.* probe.

CL. huic filium scis esse? *CH.* audivi esse in Asia. *CL.* non est, pater:

apŭd nos est. *CH.* quid ais? *CL.* advenientem, e navi egredientem ilico

abduxi ad cenam; nam mihi cum eô iam inde usque a pueritia

fûit semper familiaritas. *CH.* volŭptatem magnam nuntias.

185 quam vellem Menedemum invitatum ut nobiscum esset, amplius

ut hanc laetitiam necopinanti primus obicerem êi domi!

   atque etiam nunc tempus est. *CL.* cavĕ faxis: non opus est, pater.

CH. quapropter? *CL.* quia enim incertumst etiam quid se
faciat. modo venit;

timet omnia, patris iram et animum amicae se erga ut sit suae.

190 ëam misere amat; propter eam haec turba atque abitio evenit.
CH. scio.

CL. nunc servolum ad eam in urbem misit et ego nostrum una
Syrum.

CH. quid narrat? *CL.* quid ïlle? miserum se esse. *CH.*
miserum? quem minu' crederest?

quid relicuist quin habeat quae quidem in homine dicuntur
bona?

parentis, patriam incolumem, amicos genu' cognatos ditias.

195 atque haec perinde sunt ut illi(u)s animu' quï ea possidet:

qui uti scit êi bona; illi qui non utitur recte mala.

CL. immo ill' fuit senĕx inportunu' semper, et nunc nil magis

vereor quam nequid in illum iratu' plus satis faxit, pater.

CH. illene? (sed reprimam me: nắm in metu esse hunc illist
utile.)

200 *CL.* quid tute tecum? *CH.* dicam: ut ut erat, mansum tamen
oportuit.

fortasse aliquanto iniquior erắt praeter ei(u)s lubidinem:

pateretur; nam quem ferret si parentem non ferret suom?

huncin erat aequom ex illi(u)s more an illum ex huiu' vivere?

et quod ïllum insimulat durum id non est; nam parentum
iniuriae

205 uniu' modï sunt ferme, paullo qui est homo tolerabilis:

scortari crebro nolunt, nolunt crebro convivarier,

praebent exigue sumptum; atque haec sunt tamen ad virtutem
omnia.

verum ubi animus semel se cupiditate devinxit mala,

necessest, Clitipho, consilia consequi consimilia. hoc

210   scitumst: periclum ex aliis face[re] tibi quod ex usu siet.

    CL. ita credo. *CH.* ego ibo hinc intro, ut videam nobis quid ĭn
    cena siet.

    tŭ, ŭt tempus est diei, vidĕ sis nequo hinc abeas longius.

CLITIPHO

    CL. Quăm iniqui sunt patres in omnis adulescentis iudices!

    qui aequom esse censent nos a pueris ilico nasci senes

215   neque ĭllarum adfinis esse rerum quas fert adulescentia.

    ex suâ lubidine moderantur nunc quae est, non quae olim fuit.

    mihĭn si umquam filius erit, nĕ ĭlle facili me utetur patre;

    nam et cognoscendi et ignoscendi dabitur peccati locus:

    non ut meus, qui mihi per alium ostendit suâm sententiam.

220   perii! is mi, ubi adbibit plus paullo, sua quae narrat facinora!

    nunc ait "periclum ex aliis facito tibi quod ex usu siet":

    astutu'. nĕ ĭlle haud scit quam mihi nunc surdo narret
    fabulam.

    mage nunc me amicae dicta stimulant "da mihi" atque "adfer
    mihi":

    quoi quod respondeam nil habeo; neque me quisquamst
    miserior.

225   nam hic Clinia, etsi is quoque suarum rerum satagit, attamen

    habet bene et pudice eductam, ignaram artis meretriciae.

    meast potens procax magnifica sumptuosa nobilis.

    tum quod dem [êi] "recte" est; nam nil esse mihi religiost
    dicere.

    hoc ego mali non pridem inveni neque etiamdum scit pater.

CLINIA   CLITIPHO

230 *CLIN.* Si mihi secundae res de amore meô essent, iamdudum scio

venissent; sed vereor ne mulier me absente hic corrupta sit.

concurrunt multae opiniones quae mihi animum exaugeant:

occasio locus aetas mater quoi(u)s sub imperiost mala,

quoi nil iam praeter pretium dulcest. *CLIT.* Clinia. *CLIN.* ei misero mihi!

235 *CLIT.* etiam caves ne videat forte hic te a patre aliquis exiens?

CLIN. faciam; sed nescioquid profecto mi animu' praesagit mali.

CLIT. pergin ĭstuc priu' diiudicare quam scis quid veri siet?

CLIN. si nil mali esset iam hic adessent. *CLIT.* iam aderunt. *CLIN.* quando istuc erit?

CLIT. non cogitas hinc longule esse? et nosti mores mulierum:

240 dum moliuntur, dum conantur, annus est. *CLIN.* o Clitipho, timeo. *CLIT.* respira: eccum Dromonem cum Syro una: adsunt tibi.

SYRUS   DROMO   CLINIA   CLITIPHO

SY. Ain tu? *DR.* sic est. *SY.* verum interea, dum sermones caedimus,

illae sunt relictae. *CLIT.* mulier tibi adest. audin, Clinia?

CLIN. ego vero audio nunc demum et video et valeo, Clitipho.

245 *DR.* minime mirum: adeo inpeditae sunt: ancillarum gregem

ducunt secum. *CLIN.* perii, unde illi sunt ancillae? *CLIT.* men rogas?

SY. non oportuit relictas: portant quid rerum! *CLIN.* ei mihi!

SY. aurum vestem; et vesperascit et non noverunt viam.

factum a nobis stultest. abĭ dum tu, Dromo, illis obviam.

250   propera: quid stas? *CLIN.* vae misero mi, quanta de spe
      decidi!

    CLIT. quid ĭstuc? quae res te sollicitat autem? *CLIN.* rogitas
    quid siet?

    vidĕn tu? ancillas aurum vestem, quăm ego cum una ancillula

    hic reliqui, unde esse censes? *CLIT.* vah nunc demum
    intellego.

    SY. di boni, quid turbaest! aedes nostrae vix capient, scio.

255   quid comedent! quid ebibent! quid sene erit nostro miserius?

    sed video eccos quos volebam. *CLIN.* o Iuppiter, ubinamst
    fides?

❧ 3. *PHORMIO 1–12, 884–989*
PERIOCHA

    Chremetis frater aberat peregre Demipho

    relicto Athenis Antiphone filio.

    Chremes clam habebat Lemni uxorem et filiam,

    Athenis aliam coniugem et amantem unice

5   fidicinam gnatum. mater e Lemno advenit

    Athenas; moritur; virgo sola (aberat Chremes)

    funus procurat. ibi eam visam Antipho

    cum amaret, opera parasiti uxorem accipit.

    pater et Chremes reversi fremere. dein minas

10   triginta dant parasito, ut illam coniugem

    haberet ipse: argento hoc emitur fidicina.

    uxorem retinet Antipho a patruo adgnitam.

PHORMIO

Tantam fortunam de inproviso esse his datam!

885 summa eludendi occasiost mihi nunc senes

et Phaedriae curam adimere argentariam,

ne quoiquam suôrum aequalium supplex siet.

năm ĭdem hoc argentum, ita ut datumst, ingratiis

êi datum erit: hoc qui cogam re ipsa repperi.

890 nunc gestu' mihi voltusque est capiundus novos.

sed hinc concedam in angiportum hoc proxumum,

inde hisce ostendam me, ubi erunt egressi foras.

quo me adsimularam ire ad mercatum, non eo.

DEMIPHO   CHREMES   PHORMIO

DE. Dis magnas merito gratias habeo atque ago

895 quando evenere haec nobis, frater, prospere.

quantum potest nunc conveniundust Phormio,

priu' quam dilapidat nostras triginta minas

ut auferamu'. *PH.* Demiphonem si domist

visam ut quod ... *DE.* at nos ad te ibamu', Phormio.

900 *PH.* de eâdem hac fortasse causa? *DE.* ita hercle. *PH.* credidi:

quid ad me ibati'? *DE.* ridiculum. *PH.* verĕbamini

ne non id facerem quod recepissem semel?

heus quanta quanta haec mea paupertas est, tamen

adhuc curavi unum hoc quidem, ut mi esset fides.

905 *CH.* estne ita ut<i> dixi liberalis? *DE.* oppido.

PH. idque ad vos venio nuntiatum, Demipho,

paratum me esse: ubi voltis, uxorem date.

nam omnis posthabui mihi res, ita uti par fuit,

postquam id tanto opera vos velle animum advorteram.

910 *DE.* at hic dehŏrtatus est me nĕ ïllam tibi darem:

"nam quĭ erit rumor populi" inquit "si id feceris?

olim quom honeste potuit, tum non est data:

eam nunc extrudi turpest." ferme eadem omnia

quae tute dudum coram me incusaveras.

915 *PH.* satis superbe inluditis me. *DE.* qui? *PH.* rogas?

quia ne alteram quidem illam potero ducere;

nam quo redibo ore ad eam quam contempserim?

CH. ("tum autem Antiphonem video ab sese amittere

invitum eam" inque.) *DE.* tum autem video filium

920 invitum sane mulierem ab se amittere.

sed transi sodes ad forum atque illud mihi

argentum rursum iubĕ rescribi, Phormio.

PH. quodne ego discripsi porro illis quibu' debui?

DE. quid igitur fiet? *PH.* si vis mi uxorem dare

925 quam despondisti, ducam; sin est ut velis

manere illam apŭd te, dos hic maneat, Demipho.

nam non est aequom me propter vos decipi,

quom ego vostri honori' causa repudium alterae

remiserim, quae doti' tantundem dabat.

930 *DE.* in' hinc malam rem cŭm ïstac magnificentia,

fugitive? etiamnunc credi' te ignorarier

aut tua facta adeo? *PH.* irritor. *DE.* tune hanc duceres

si tibi daretur? *PH.* fac periclum. *DE.* ut filius

cŭm ïlla habitet apŭd te, hoc vostrum consilium fuit.

935 *PH.* quaeso quid narras? *DE.* quin tu mi argentum cedo.

PH. ïmmŏ vero uxorem tu cedo. *DE.* in ius ambula.

[in ius]   *PH.* enĭmvero si porro esse odiosi pergitis . . .

DE. quid facies? *PH.* egone? vos me indotatis modo

patrocinari fortasse arbitramini:

940   etiam dotatis soleo. *CH.* quid ĭd nostra? *PH.* nihil.

hic quandam noram quoi(u)s vir uxorem   *CH.* hem. *DE.* quid
   est?

PH. Lemni habuit aliam, *CH.* nullu' sum. *PH.* exqua filiam

suscepit; et eam clam educat. *CH.* sepultu' sum.

PH. haec adeo ego illi iam denarrabo. *CH.* obsecro,

945   ne facias. *PH.* oh tune is eras? *DE.* ut ludos facit!

CH. missum te facimu'. *PH.* fabulae! *CH.* quid vis tibi?

argentum quod habes condonamu' te. *PH.* audio.

quid vos, malum, ergo me sic ludificamini

inepti vostra puerili sententia?

950   nolo volo; volŏ nolo rursum; cape cedo;

quod dictum indictumst; quod modo erat ratum inritumst.

CH. quo pacto aut unde hic haec rescivit? *DE.* nescio;

nisi me dixisse nemini certo scio.

CH. monstri, ita me dĭ ament, simile. *PH.* inieci scrupulum.
   DE. hem

955   hicine ut a nobis hoc tantum argenti auferat

tam aperte inridens? emori hercle satius est.

animo virili praesentique ut sis para.

vides peccatum tuom | esse elatum foras

neque iam id celare posse te uxorem tuam:

960   nunc quod ĭpsa ex aliis auditura sit, Chreme,

id nosmet indicare placabilius est.

tum hunc inpuratum poterimus nostro modo

ulciscī. *PH.* attat nisi mi prospicio, haereo.

hi gladiatorio animo ad me adfectant viam.

965 CH. at vereor ut placari possit. DE. bono animo es:

ego redigam vos in gratiam, hoc fretus, Chreme,

quom e medio excessit unde haec susceptast tibi.

PH. itan agiti' mecum? satis astute adgredimini.

non hercle ex rĕ ĭsti(u)s me instigasti, Demipho.

970 ain tu? ubi quae lubitum fuerit peregre feceris

neque hui(u)s sis veritu' feminae primariae

quin novŏ modo ei faceres contumeliam,

venias nunc precibu' lautum peccatum tuom?

hisce ego ĭllam dictis ita tibi incensam dabo

975 ut ne restinguas lacrumis si exstillaveris.

DE. malum quod isti di deaeque omnes duint!

tantane adfectum quemquam esse hominem audacia!

non hoc publicitu' scelus hinc asportarier

in solas terras! CH. in ĭd redactu' sum loci

980 ut quid agam cŭm ĭllo nesciam prorsum. DE. ego scio:

in ius eamus. PH. in ius? huc, siquid lubet.

CH. adsequere, retine dum ego huc servos evoco.

DE. enĭm nequeo solus: accurre. PH. una iniuriast

tecum. DE. lege agito ergo. PH. alterast tecum, Chreme.

985 CH. rape hunc. PH. sic agitis? enĭmvero vocest opus:

Nausistrata, exi! CH. os opprime inpurum: vide

quantum valet. PH. Nausistrata! inquam. DE. non taces?

PH. taceam? DE. nisi sequitur, pugnos in ventrem ingere.

PH. vel oculum exclude: est ubi vos ulciscar probe.

❧ 4. *HECYRA 198–280*

LACHES   SOSTRATA

LA. Pro deum ătque hominum fidem, quod hŏc genus est,
quaĕ haĕc est coniuratio!

utin omnes mulieres eadem aeque studeant nolintque omnia

200 neque declinatam quicquam ab aliarum ingenio ullam
reperias!

itaque adeo uno animo omnes socrŭs oderunt nurus.

virïs esse advorsas aeque studiumst, simili' pertinaciast,

in eodemque omnes mihi videntur ludo doctae ad malitiam; et

êi ludo, si ullus est, magistram hanc esse sati' certo scio.

205   *SO.* me miseram, quae nunc quăm ŏb rem accuser
nescio. *LA.* hem

tu nescis? *SO.* non, ita me di bene ament, mi Lache,

itaque una inter nos agere aetatem liceat. *LA.* di mala
prohibeant.

SO. meque abs te inmerito esse accusatam post modo
rescisces. *LA.* scio,

te inmerito? an quicquam pro istis factis dignum te dici
potest?

210 quae mĕ ĕt tĕ ĕt familiam dedecoras, filio luctum paras;

tum autem ex amicis inimici ut sint nobis adfines facis,

qui illum decrerunt dignum suôs quoi liberos committerent.

tu sola exorere quae perturbes haec tua inpudentia.

SO. egŏn? *LA.* tŭ ïnquam, mulier, quae me omnino lapidem,
non hominem putas.

215 an, quia ruri esse crebro soleo, nescire arbitramini

quo quisque pacto hic vitam vostrarum exigat?

multo melius hic quae fiunt quam illi[c] ubi sum adsidue scio.

ideo quia, ŭt vos mihi domi eriti', proinde ego ero fama foris.

iampridem equidem audivi cepisse odium tuî Philumenam,

220 minimeque adeo [est] mirum, et nĭ ĭd fecisset mage mirum
     foret;

sed non credidi adeo ut etiam totam hanc odisset domum:

quod si scissem illa hic maneret potiu', tŭ hĭnc isses foras.

at vidĕ quam inmerito aegritudo haec oritur mi abs te, Sostrata:

rus habitatum abii concedens vobis et reî serviens,

225 sumptus vostros otiumque ut nostra res posset pati,

meô labori haud parcens praeter aequom atque aetatem meam.

non te pro his curasse rebu' nequid aegre esset mihi!

SO. non mea opera neque pol culpa evenit. *LA.* immo
     maxume:

sola hic fuîsti: in tĕ ŏmnis haeret culpa sola, Sostrata.

230 quae hic erant curares, quom ego vos curis solvi ceteris.

cum puella anum suscepisse inimicitias non pudet?

illi(u)s dices culpa factum? *SO.* haud equidem dico, mi Lache.

LA. gaudeo, ita me dĭ ament, gnati causa; nam de te quidem

sati' scio peccando detrimenti nil fieri potest.

235 *SO.* qui scis an ea causa, mi vir, me odisse adsimulaverit

ut cum matre plus una esset? *LA.* quid ais? non signi hoc sat
     est,

quod herĭ nemo voluit visentem ad eam te intro admittere?

SO. enĭm lassam oppido tum esse aîbant: eo ad eam non
     admissa sum.

LA. tuôs esse ego ĭlli mores morbum mage quam ullam aliam
     rem arbitror,

240 et merito adeo; nam vostrarum nullast quin gnatum velit

ducere uxorem; et quae vobis placitast condicio datur:

ubi duxere inpulsu vostro, vostro inpulsu eâsdem exigunt.

PHIDIPPUS   LACHES   SOSTRATA

PH. Etsi scio ego, Philumenă, meûm ius esse ut te cogam

quae ego imperem facere, ego tamen patrio animo victu'
   faciam

245 ut tibi concedam neque tuae lubidini advorsabor.

LA. atque eccum Phidippum optume video: hinc iam scibo
   hoc quid sit.

Phidippe, etsi ego meîs me omnibus scio ĕsse adprime
   obsequentem,

sed non adeo ut mea facilitas corrumpat illorum animos:

quod tu si idem faceres, magis in rĕm ĕt vostram et nostram id
   esset.

250 nunc video in illarum potestate esse te. PH. heia vero.

LA. adii te heri de filia: ut veni, itidem incertum amisti.

haud ita decet, si perpetuam hanc vis esse adfinitatem,

celare te iras. siquid est peccatum a nobis profer:

aut ea refellendo aut purgando vobis corrigemus

255 te iudice ipso. sin east causa retinendi apud vos

quia aegrast, te mihi ĭniuriam facere arbitror, Phidippe,

si metui' satis ut meaĕ domi curetur diligenter.

at ita me dĭ ament, haud tibi hoc concedo—[etsi] illi pateres—

ut tŭ ĭllam salvam mage velis quam ego: id adeo gnati causa,

260 quem ego intellexi illam haud minus quam se ipsum magni
   facere.

neque adeo clam me est quăm ĕsse eum graviter laturum
   credam,

hoc si rescierit: eô domum studeo haec priu' quam ille redeat.

PH. Laches, et diligentiam vostram et benignitatem

novi et quae dicis omnia esse ut dicis animum induco,

265 et te hoc mihi cupio credere: illam ad vos redire studeo

si facere possim ullo modo. *LA.* quae res te id facere prohibet?

eho num quid nam accusat virum? *PH.* minime. nam
   postquam attendi

magis et vi coepi cogere ut rediret, sancte adiurat

non posse apud vos Pamphilo se absente perdurare.

270 aliud fortasse aliis viti est: ego sum animo leni natus:

non possum advorsari meis. *LA.* em Sostrata. *SO.* heu me
   miseram!

LA. certumne est istuc? *PH.* nunc quidem ut videtur: sed
   num quid vis?

nam est quod me transire ad forum iam oportet. *LA.* eo
   tecum una.

SOSTRATA

SO. Edepol ne nos sumus inique aeque omnes invisae viris

275 propter paucas, quae omnes faciunt dignae ut videamur malo.

nam ita me dï ament, quod me accusat nunc vir, sum extra
   noxiam.

sed non facile est expurgatu: ita animum induxerunt socrus

omnis esse iniquas: haud pol mequidem; nam numquam secus

habui illam ac si ex më ësset gnata, nec quï höc mi eveniat scio;

280 nisi pol filium multimodis iam exspecto ut redeat domum.

❧ 5. *EUNUCHUS Didascalia, 539–614*
DIDASCALIA

INCIPIT EVNUCHVS TERENTI: ACTA LVDIS MEGA-
LENSIBVS L . POSTVMIO ALBINO L . CORNELIO MERVLA
AEDILIBVS CVRVLIBVS: EGERE L . AMBIVIVS TVRPIO
L . ATILIVS PRAENESTINVS: MODOS FECIT FLACCVS

CLAVDI TIBIIS DVABVS DEXTRIS: GRAECA MENAN-
DRV: FACTA II M . VALERIO C . FANNIO COS.

ANTIPHO

AN. Heri aliquot adulescentuli coiimus in Piraeo

540   in hunc diem, ut de symbolis essemu'. Chaeream eî reî

praefecimus; dati anuli; locu' tempu' constitutumst.

praeteriit tempu': quo in loco dictumst parati nil est;

homo ipse nusquamst neque scio quid dicam aut quid
coniectem.

nunc mi hoc negoti ceteri dedere ut illum quaeram

545   idque adeo visam si domist. quisnam hinc ab Thaide exit?

is est an non est? ipsus est. quid hŏc hominist? quĭ hic
ornatust?

quid ïllud malist? nequeo satis mirari neque conicere;

nisi, quidquid est, procul hinc lubet priu' quid sit sciscitari.

CHAEREA   ANTIPHO

CH. Numquis hic est? nemost. numquis hinc me sequitur?
nemo homost.

550   iamne erumpere hoc licet mi gaudium? pro Iuppiter,

nunc est profecto interfici quom perpeti me possum,

ne hoc gaudium contaminet vita aegritudine aliqua.

sed neminemne curiosum intervenire nunc mihi

qui me sequatur quoquo eam, rogitando obtundat enicet

555   quid gestiam aut quid laetu' sim, quo pergam, unde emergam,
ubi siem

vestitum hunc nanctu', quid mi quaeram, sanu' sim anne
insaniam!

AN. adibo atque ab eo gratiam hanc, quam video velle, inibo.

Chaerea, quid ĕst quod sic gestis? quid sibi hic vestitu'
quaerit?

quid ĕst quod laetus es? quid tibi vis? satine sanu's? quid me
adspectas?

560   quid taces? *CH.* o festu' dies hominis! amice, salve:

nemost hominum quem ego nunc magis cuperem videre
quam te.

AN. narra istuc quaeso quid sit. *CH.* immo ego te obsecro
hercle ut audias.

nostin hanc quăm amat frater? *AN.* novi: nempe, opinor,
Thaidem.

CH. istam ipsam. *AN.* sic commemineram. *CH.* quaedam
hodie est êi dono data

565   virgo: quid ego ĕiu' tibi nunc faciem praedicem aut laudem,
Antipho,

quom ipsum me noris quam elegans formarum spectator siem?

in hac commotu' sum. *AN.* âin tu? *CH.* primam dices, sciŏ,
si videris.

quid multa verba? amare coepi. forte fortuna domi

erăt quidam eunuchu' quem mercatu' fuerat frater Thaidi,

570   neque is deductus etiamdum ad eam. submonuit me Parmeno

ibi servo' quod ego arripui. *AN.* quid id est? *CH.* tacitu' citius
audies:

ut vestem cŭm ĭllo mutem et pro illo iubeam mĕ illoc ducier.

AN. pro eunuchon? *CH.* sic est. *AN.* quid ĕx ea re tandem ut
caperes commodi?

CH. rogas? viderem audirem essem una quacum cupiebam,
Antipho.

575   num parva causa aut prava ratiost? traditus sum mulieri.

illa ilico ubi me accepit, laeta vero ad se abducit domum;

commendat virginem. *AN.* quoi? tibine? *CH.* mihi. *AN.*
satis tuto tamen?

CH. edicit ne vir quisquam ad eam adeat et mihi ne abscedam
imperat;

in interiore parti ut maneam solu' cum sola. adnuo

580 terram intuens modeste. *AN.* miser. *CH.* "ego" inquit "ad
cenam hinc eo."

abducit secum ancillas: paucae quae circum illam essent
manent

noviciae puellae. continuo haec adornant ut lavet.

adhortor properent. dum adparatur, virgo in conclavi sedet

suspectans tabulam quandam pictam: ibi inerat pictura haec,
Iovem

585 quo pacto Danaae misisse aiunt quondam in gremium imbrem
aureum.

egomet quoque id spectare coepi, et quia consimilem luserat

iam olim ille ludum, inpendio magis animu' gaudebat mihi,

deŭm sese in hominem convortisse atque in alienas tegulas

venisse clanculum per ïnpluvium fucum factum mulieri.

590 at quem deum! "qui templa caeli summa sonitu concutit."

ego homuncio hoc non facerĕm? ego ïllud vero ita fecī—ac
lubens.

dum haec mecum reputo, accersitur lavatum interea virgo:

iit lavit rediit; deinde eam in lecto illae conlocarunt.

stŏ ĕxspectans siquid mi imperent. venit una, "heus tu" inquit
"Dore,

595 cape hoc flabellum, ventulum huic sic facito, dum lavamur:

ubi nos laverimu', si voles, lavato." accipio tristis.

AN. tum equidem istuc os tuom inpudens videre nimium
vellem,

quï ĕsset status, flabell<ul>um tenere te asinum tantum.

CH. vix elocutast hoc, foras simul omnes proruont se,

600 abeunt lavatum, perstrepunt, ita ut fit domini ubi absunt.

interea somnu' virginem opprimīt. ego limis specto

sic per flabellum clanculum; simul alia circumspecto,

satin explorata sint. video esse. pessulum ostio obdo.

AN. quid tum? *CH.* quid "quid tum," fatue? *AN.* fateor.
   CH. an ego occasionem

605 mi ostentam, tantam, tam brevem, tam optatam, tam
   insperatam

amitterem? tum pol ego is essem vero qui simulabar.

AN. sane hercle ut dici'. sed ïnterim de symbolis quid
   actumst?

CH. paratumst. *AN.* frugi es: ubi? domin? *CH.* immo apŭd
   libertum Discum.

AN. perlongest, sed tanto ocius properemu': muta vestem.

610 *CH.* ubi mutem? perii; nam domo exsulo nunc: metuo
   fratrem

ne intus sit; porro autem pater ne rure redierit iam.

AN. eamus ad me, ibi proxumumst ubi mutes. *CH.* recte dicis.

eamus; et de istac simul, quo pacto porro possim

potiri, consilium volo capere una tecum. *AN.* fiat.

❧ 6. *ADELPHOE 1–25, 787–881*
PROLOGUS

Postquam poeta sensit scripturam suam

ab iniquis observari, et advorsarios

rapere in peiorem partem quam acturi sumus,

indicio de se ipse erĭt, vos eritis iudices

5 laudin an vitio duci factum oporteat.

Synapothnescontes Diphili comoediast:

êam Commorientis Plautu' fecit fabulam.

in Graeca adulescens est qui lenoni eripit

meretricem in prima fabula: êum Plautus locum

10 reliquit integrum, êum hic locum sumpsit sibi

in Adelphos, verbum de verbo expressum extulit.

êam nos acturi sumu' novam: pernoscite

furtumne factum existumetis an locum

reprehensum qui praeteritu' neglegentiast.

15 nam quod ïsti dicunt malevoli, homines nobilis

hunc adiutare adsidueque una scribere,

quod ïlli maledictum vehemens esse existumant,

êam laudem hic ducit maxumam quom illis placet

qui vobis univorsis et populo placent,

20 quorum opera in bello in otio in negotio

suô quisque tempore usust sine superbia.

de(h)inc ne exspectetis argumentum fabulae,

senes qui primi venient î partem aperient,

in agendo partem ostendent. facite aequanimitas

25 poetae ad scribendum augeat industriam.

MICIO   DEMEA

MI. Parata a nobis sunt, ita ŭt dixi, Sostrata:

ubi vis . . . quisnam a me pepulit tam graviter fores?

DE. ei mihi! quid faciam? quid agam? quid clamem aut
    querar?

790 "o caelum, o terra, o maria Neptuni!" *MI.* em tibi!

rescivit omnem rem: id nunc clamat: ilicet;

paratae lites: succurrendumst. *DE.* eccum adest

communi' corruptela nostrum liberum.

MI. tandem reprime iracundiam atque ad te redi.

795 *DE.* repressi redii, mitto maledicta omnia:

rěm ĭpsam putemu'. dictum hoc inter nos fuit

(ex tě adeo ortumst) ne tu curares meum

neve ego tuom? responde. *MI.* factumst, non nego.

DE. quor nunc apud te potat? quor recipis meum?

800 quor emis amicam, Micio? numqui minus

mihi idem ius aequomst esse? quid mecumst tibi?

quando ego tuom non curo, ne cura meum.

MI. non aequom dici'. *DE.* non? *MI.* nam vetu' verbum hoc quidemst,

communia esse amicorum inter se omnia.

805 *DE.* facete! nunc demum istaec nata oratiost?

MI. ausculta paucis nisi molestumst, Demea.

principio, si id te mordet, sumptum filii

quem faciunt, quaeso hoc facito tecum cogites:

tŭ ĭllos duo olim pro re tolerabas tua,

810 quod sati' putabas tua bona ambobus fore,

et me tum uxorem credidisti scilicet

ducturum. eandem illam rationem antiquam optine:

conserva quaere parce, fac quam plurumum

illis relinquas, gloriam tŭ ĭstam optine.

815 mea, quae praeter spem evenere, utantur sine.

de summa nil decedet: quod hĭnc accesserit

id de lucro putato esse omne. haec si voles

in animo vere cogitare, Demea,

et mihi et tibi et illis dempseris molestiam.

820 *DE.* mitto rem: consuetudinem amborum ... *MI.* mane:

scio; istuc ibam. multa in homine, Demea,

signa insunt ex quibu' coniectura facile fit,

duo quŏm idem faciunt saepe, ut possis dicere

"hoc licet inpune facere huic, illi non licet,"

825 non quo dissimili' res sit sed quŏ ĭs qui facit.

quaĕ ego inesse illis video, ut confidam fore

ita ŭt volumu'. video [eôs] sapere intellegere, in loco

vereri, inter se amare: scire est liberum

ingenium atque animum: quovis illos tu die

830 redducas. at enĭm metuas nĕ ăb re sint tamen

omissiores paullo. o noster Demea,

ad omnia alia aetate sapimus rectius;

solum unum hoc vitium adfert senectus hominibus:

adtentiores sumus ad rem omnes quam sat est:

835 quod ĭllos sat aetas acuet. *DE.* ne nimium modo

bonae tuae istae nos rationes, Micio,

et tuos iste animus aequo' subvortat. *MI.* tace:

non fiet. mitte iăm ĭstaec; da te hodie mihi:

exporge frontem. *DE.* scilicet ita tempu' fert:

840 faciundumst. ceterum ego rus cras cum filio

cum primo luci ibo hinc. *MI.* de nocte censeo:

hodie modo hilarum te face. *DE.* et ĭstam psaltriam

una illuc mecum hinc abstraham. *MI.* pugnaveris:

eŏ pacto prorsum illi adligaris filium.

845 modo facito ut illam serves. *DE.* ego ĭstuc videro,

atque ibi favillae plena, fumi ac pollinis

coquendo sit faxo et molendo; praeter haec

meridie ipso faciam ut stipulam colligat:

tăm ĕxcoctam reddam atque atram quam carbost. *MI.* placet:

850   nunc mihi videre sapere. atque equidem filium

tum, etiam si nolit, cogam ut cŭm ïlla una cubet.

DE. derides? fortunatu's qui isto animo sies.

ego sentio ... *MI.* ah pergisne? *DE.* iam iam desino.

MI. ï ĕrgo intro, et quoi reîst eî reî [hilarum] hunc sumamus
diem.

DEMEA

855   *DE.* Numquam ita quisquam bene subducta ratione ad vitam
fuit

quin res aetas usu' semper aliquid adportet novi,

aliquid moneat: ut ïlla quae te scisse credas nescias,

et quae tibi putaris prima, in experiundo ut repudies.

quod nunc me evenit; nam ego vitam duram quam vixi usque
adhuc

860   iam decurso spatio omitto. id quăm ŏb rem? re ipsa repperi

facilitate nil esse homini meliu' neque clementia.

id ĕsse verum ex mĕ ătque ex fratre quoivis facilest noscere.

ill' suâm semper egit vitam in otio, in conviviis,

clemens placidu', nulli laedere os, adridere omnibus;

865   sibi vixit, sibi sumptum fecit: omnes bene dicunt, amant.

ego ille agresti' saevo' tristi' parcu' truculentus tenax

duxi uxorem: quam ibi miseriam vidi! nati filii,

alia cura. heia autem, dum studeo illis ut quam plurumum

facerem, contrivi in quaerundo vitam atque aetatem meam:

870   nunc exacta aetate hoc fructi pro labore ab eis fero,

odium; ille alter sine labore patria potitur commoda.

illum amant, me fugitant; illi credunt consilia omnia,

illum diligunt, apud illum sunt ambo, ego desertu' sum;

illum ut vivat optant, meam autem mortem exspectant scilicet.

875 ita eos meŏ labore eductos maxumo hic fecit suos

paullo sumptu: miseriam omnem ego capio, hic potitur gaudia.

age age, nunciam experiamur contra ecquid ego possiem

blande dicere aut benigne facere, quando hoc provocat.

ego quoque a meis me amari et magni pendi postulo:

880 si id fit dando atque obsequendo, non posteriores feram.

deerit: id meă minime refert qui sum natu maxumus.

Commentary

⌘ *ANDRIA, Terence's First Play, 166 BCE*
Starting the Plot

In this play, Terence starts from almost nothing and gradually builds up characters and dramatic background until in the final lines he clears away doubts and misinformation and makes a postponed wedding work. The canceled wedding is the first event to be explained, by the angry father of Pamphilus. Simo, the disgusted father, has learned his facts by spying on his son, and he has many of the details incorrect. Yet his is the authoritative voice of the narrative introduction. Terence gets us to question the information supplied by Simo, and ignorance is far from bliss in this comedy, as in later creations of this playwright. Two house-fronts are visible, one belonging to affluent Athenian Simo, the other to the Andrian woman, a foreigner and courtesan. Enter Simo, Sosia, his freedman, and two slaves carrying materials for a dinner. Simo speaks first. Terence moves carefully to sketch the background and early complications of his plot.

28   **vos** He addresses the slaves, sending them indoors, while he stays with Sosia.

      istaec points to their cooking things. *istae* for *ista,* n. acc. pl. The final *c* adds the sense of "here" to the pronoun. The slaves pick up their goods and, at the second command of Simo, move quickly into his house.

29   **ades dum.** the first word is pres. imperative, slightly modulated by *dum,* an enclitic. Sosia has started off with the slaves when recalled.

paucis (i.e., *verbis*). Abl. "for a few words." But he guesses wrongly at the reason and smartly tells Simo to consider his words said and understood.

30   **nempe** "obviously you mean that this meal should be done well." From this, we can infer that Sosia appears as a cook, in charge of the slaves. Simo corrects Sosia and stresses "something else."

31   **ars.** Cooks proudly talked of their "art" in those days, too.

32   **arte** abl. with **opus est**. Simo denies interest in the dinner.

Istac abl. + *c*; cf. above 28.

33   **eis** (i.e., *artibus*). Same construction in abl.

34   Simo values loyalty and silence, useful virtues in a servant. Sosia is puzzled by (*quid velis*) the way the situation has developed, and that leads into Simo's narrative which provides background details for Sosia and the audience.

35   **te emi** We learn that from an early age (*a parvolo = parvulo*) Sosia was a slave bought by Simo for the household, not for hard field service.

36   Simo represents himself as a model master. **Fuerit:** pf. subjunctive in indirect question.

37   The position of the first word demands Sosia's agreement. Simo freed Sosia at a relatively young age. **Esses:** impf. subjunctive in a noun clause depending on *feci ut.*

38   **servibas** = *serviebas*

liberaliter Terence likes to use this adv. to refer to natural freedom, observed in the manners of a slave.

39   Simo stresses the supreme value of what he gave his slave, but the value was to Sosia: Simo had many other things of greater value to himself.

40   Sosia has words of gratitude forced from him, and Simo confirms again his noble generosity.

41   **quid** indefinite form of *aliquid* after *si*

43-45 Sosia resents the feeling he gets that Simo is beating around the bush, to suggest doubts about his loyal gratitude. Notice the echo of *gratum* and *gratiam*. What is he driving at? In quite formal Latin, Sosia protests; Terence assigns him the earliest surviving uses of the two verbal nouns *commemoratio* and *exprobatio*.

Inmemoris obj. gen. with the preceding word and responsible for the obj.gen. of the next.

Quin . . . dic why not tell me?

Velis Supply *facere*.

46-47 **nuptiae** This is the first we have heard of a wedding, a key detail. We can now reconstruct the opening situation: Sosia was, he thought, coming to Simo's home to cook a wedding dinner. But now already we are learning that the wedding is a pretense. Simo controls the pretense.

48 **quor** = *cur*. Terence links the name of Simo with simulation.

49-50 Simo's plot has to do with his son and has a role for Sosia.

51-52 Between the ages of eighteen and twenty, Athenian males were classified as ephebes and were subject to military training. Once the ephebe period was over, young men started to plan their lives and test their freedom. The name of the son we finally learn in 90 is Pamphilus, a frequently-used name that suggests vulnerability to love, a regular subject of this type of comedy. Line 52 is marked corrupt with a symbol called an "obelos," but its sense seems obvious and otiose: at twenty, a young man enjoys some freedom.

52-54 The parenthetical statement, to which Sosia assents, argues that the character of a young man does not clearly show itself so long as he is under the authority of his elders and teachers, those he owes respect.

55-57 Simo reviews the typical behavior of an ex-ephebe. Some personal interest or passion starts to dominate his time and slowly define him as an individual. Horse-racing, hunting with dogs, and attending lectures of philosophers are all put on a level, which may say more about Simo than his son.

aut equos alere aut canes The infinitive is understood as doubled with the two different objects, each unit in apposition with *studium*. *aut ad philosophos* does not pick up *ad venandum*, but refers back to *ad aliquod studium*.

58-59 Pamphilus had no special interest in these things, and he participated in them moderately.

mediocriter placed emphatically by Simo, who values moderation perhaps more than he should.

60-61 When Simo voices his pleasure in his son's moderation, Sosia chimes in with a tired old Greek commonplace: "do nothing in excess." The Latin version starts a subjunctive clause, but omits the verb (i.e., *agas*).

62-65 Simo summarizes the "life" of his son in a series of infinitive clauses. First, he tolerated everyone (*omnis* acc. pl.) without favoritism. However, when he was with any particular persons, he threw himself into their passions.

quibus . . . quomque tmesis. He would follow their interests almost slavishly, and he never opposed anyone or put his own desires ahead of theirs. *is = eis*; *facillume = facillime*.

66-68 Simo concludes this portrait of his son by telling Sosia (hence 2nd pers. sing.) that the boy earned popularity (without envy) and gained (*pares* pres. subjunctive) friends. He is proud of his son's calculated moderation. Sosia replies with enthusiastic assent. Pamphilus acted wisely in accordance with the times. Sosia loyally parrots his former master on the value of *obsequium* (cf. 64) in winning friends and the contrasting result of dislike that results from truth, i.e., talking honestly to people. Here, Terence makes his audience feel uneasy about Simo's and Sosia's reasoning. And many recognized that the pair are unwise about what they call Pamphilus' "wisdom." Cicero, an admirer and frequent citer of Terence, in *De Amicitia* 89 made it quite clear that the true ideal of friendship was loyal frankness or "truth"; that deliberate *obsequium* encouraged friends to follow a destructive course. The commentator Donatus confirms Cicero by reporting that wise men criticized Sosia's words when they commented on line 68. This ends the first part of Simo's report on Pamphilus' lifestyle, and we are to see that he is an unreliable narrator from the start.

69-70 The second sequence introduces the temptation of love for the young man and Simo's ineffective guardianship of Pamphilus. The house next door, now for the first time called to our attention, has been acquired by a woman who has moved here from the island of Andros.

viciniae The text is disputed in the manuscripts because of the difficult grammar. It means: "to this neighborhood."

71-73 The details give a stereotyped picture of the making of a prostitute but Terence is sympathetic, not hostile. He describes a beautiful young girl, *aetate integra* ("in the prime of life") forced by poverty and negligent relatives to seek a living in wealthy Athens. Sosia immediately regards her as a threat to the model Pamphilus, and he invites us to identify her as the title-role of the play. The exclamation *ei* at 73 stresses his fear (cf. 106).

adportet subjunctive in a clause after a verb of fearing

mali partitive gen. after *ne (ali-)quid*

74-75 The three adverbs of 74 emphasize the fact that the Andrian started off in "honest" woman's work. She tried to earn a living weaving wool. This is the proverbial honest labor of a good woman in Rome.

76-79 A would-be lover tried to seduce her by a tempting amount of money. Others tried, too.

hominum not "men," but human beings and referring here to the girl. Simo generalizes again: people are inclined to leave off labor for lust. That does not reflect much sympathy from Simo. At any rate, the Andrian gave up her weaving and accepted the arrangement proposed, and thus began to earn her living as a courtesan or prostitute.

quaestum a business earning money; often applies specifically to prostitution

80-82 The young friends of Pamphilus, who visited the Andrian often together, would take him along, no doubt offering him a chance to employ her, too. And Simo quickly leapt to the conclusion that his boy was caught in the trap. Notice that father and son never talk the situation over, and all Simo's information and misinformation come from talking to others.

83-85 **habet** a gladiatorial term, equivalent to our "he has it" or "has had it" (meaning a deadly wound, here of love). Simo spies on the house of the courtesan and spots the slaves of his son's friends. Without thinking to talk to Pamphilus, he approaches the slaves and trusts them more than his son (*heus*—"hey," *sodes*—"if you will").

86-89 The slaves named one or another of Pamphilus' friends as the lover, but Pamphilus' name never came up. The second part of 87 is very awkward, but has not been solved by scholars. Hence, another obelos (cf.52). Finally, the impatient Simo asked pointedly (as implied by exclam. *eho)* about his son. Answer: he just dined with his friends.

symbolam dedit He paid his share of agreed-upon expenses for the food. We will find that the slaves conspire to keep Simo ignorant. In his ignorant gratification, Simo is delighted with his son. We are fooled, too.

90-92 To make sure, Simo asks again on another day and receives the same heartening answer. *comperibam* = *comperiebam* (cf. 38).

spectatum satis sufficiently tested and proved, by what the slaves responded. Not a foolproof test. But it is enough to send Simo into irrational raptures. His son is a paradigm of restraint.

putabam impf. tense indicates that in time Simo might change his mind, as he does.

93-95 Simo again solemnly explains his thinking based on experience.

conflictatur perhaps simply "associates with," but the military metaphor occurs probably to Simo, who views Pamphilus as a hero. Hence "struggles with."

96-98 **quom . . . tum** correlative clauses, with the archaic *quom* for later Latin *cum*. There are two infinitives controlling clauses in the *tum*-section. They could be historical infinitives or subjects also of *placebat*. Terence here stresses the egotistic pride of Simo.

qui . . . haberem subjunctive to emphasize that this is what others said, not a provable fact

99-102 **verbis** another abl. with *opus est*. Loquacious Simo continues his narrative, always from his mistaken viewpoint. The result of Pamphilus' high reputation is that a wealthy friend named Chremes proposes marriage between his only daughter and Simo's son. The fathers agree, and the wedding is set for today.

103-5 Sosia raises the question that should have occurred to Terence's audience. In 47, Simo had warned Sosia that he was not cooking for a real marriage. Why not? Simo postpones his answer and instead brings up a new detail: neighbor Chrysis has suddenly died. That does not answer the question, but rather seems to complicate it. However, loyal Sosia immediately responds with a congratulatory cheer. If Chrysis is the Andrian of the title, and we are still early in Act I, this play should come to an end. And it obviously does not.

106-9 Still not talking to Pamphilus, Simo watches him like a hawk and interprets his grief to suit his expectations. Pamphilus takes an active and humane role in the funeral arrangements. And Simo thoroughly approves.

110-12 Again he explains his thinking and reveals more of his egotism.

huiu' The apostrophe indicates an *s*, dropped to gain a short syllable (cf. *eiu'* 115).

amasset Contracted form of plpf. subjunctive. Terence helps his meter by dropping *-vi-*.

parvae consuetudinis "slight relationship." Simo is sure of this because of his talking with the slaves.

fert familiariter Pamphilus seems to act, as we would say, "like a member of the family." But all this leads to the selfish conclusion of Simo: if he grieves so over an insignificant woman, what will he do when Simo, his own father, dies?

113-14 **putabam** Again, as in 92, impf. tense suggests that Simo will change his opinion.

mansueti "kindly." Again, Simo, who has not answered Sosia's nor our question, calls attention to his verbosity.

115-16 **eius causa** "for his (Pamphilus') sake." This phrase covers a lot of possible reasons. Simo had no valid excuse to attend this funeral. He plants the word *mali*, which marks the dramatic change in his story, from happy to evil. Sosia echoes the new mood with an anxious *hem* ("uh oh").

117-20 The friends of Chrysis have gathered at her house, where her corpse is laid out on a bier. The funeral begins when the bier is carried from the house, and the friends follow it in a procession. Simo takes a position in the procession from which he can see as much as possible. So he spots a young woman he has never seen before who needs some of description. After starting with a noun, he hesitates over the appropriate adj., which then Sosia quickly supplies (*bona*).

ut nil supra no face could surpass it. The verb for a result clause suggests itself.

121-24 **honesta ac liberali** these adjectives suggest a natural superiority that goes with free birth. This girl in fact is freeborn, not a slave or a courtesan. Busy Simo quickly starts asking around of the slaves of Chrysis, everyone but his son, who she is. Since she is the sister of Chrysis, that leaves her open to be the Andrian of the title.

125-26 **percussit** subject is the identification of the sister or an impersonal "it." Simo has suddenly gotten close to the true picture of things.

attat an exclamatory word such as "aha." Not the dead Chrysis, but the living and lovely sister is the cause of Pamphilus' tears and tenderness.

127-29 Sosia expresses his anxiety about where these details are leading. Back to the funeral, whose procession has reached the tomb and the pyre, which is set up nearby. A series of short clauses summarizes the action. When the corpse is placed on the burning pyre, everyone weeps.

130-33 The girl gets dangerously close to the fire. Afraid for her safety, Pamphilus betrays himself and the love that, according to Simo, he has skillfully "dissimulated" and concealed. Note the word "dissimulation" in the mouth and thoughts of Simo again.

134-36 These are the first words attributed to Pamphilus, and he does not even speak them on stage.

mea Glycerium The form of the name is neuter, but Glycerium is obviously feminine. Pamphilus' wildness and the possessive adj. leave no doubt that they are lovers.

perditum acc. of the supine, with a verb of motion (*is*). Simo has seen enough to grasp the feelings of Pamphilus. It remains to prove that the girl feels the same toward him. Notice the new relevance of *familiariter* (cf. 111).

137 Sosia expresses himself in an astounded question to Simo's words. Then in our final line Simo reacts to this new crisis. He has obviously changed from a proud to angry father.

∾ HEAUTON, *Terence's* SELF-TORMENTOR, 163 BCE

Complications

I translate the Greek title, which is *Heauton Timorumenos*. Terence started his play in a scene involving two older men, Menedemus and Chremes, nextdoor neighbors. Each has a son in a different type of love affair. The main purpose of the opening scene, as in the *Andria*, which we have just read, was to have Menedemus narrate to Chremes a major portion of the background. Menedemus punishes himself for driving his son Clinia away from home to make himself a responsible citizen. He has been away now about six months, torn from the passionate love affair he was leading with a poor girl named Antiphi-la. We also hear the patronizing attitude of Chremes, who does not talk about his own son and knows nothing of his indulgence with a prostitute Bacchis who is a real gold-digger. It is the purpose of this second section of the comedy to fill us in on Chremes' son Clitipho and to develop a contrast between the fathers and sons and the girls that they love. We start with Clitipho and domineering Chremes. Clitipho enters from his house, finishing a conversation he has been having with Clinia, the other lover, whom everybody supposes is still far away abroad. In fact, Clinia couldn't keep up the separation from Antiphila and has sneaked back to Athens, where Clitipho has met him and hidden him in his own home.

175-77 **quod vereare**: subjunctive in relative purpose clause. Clinia's "fear" is his anxious distrust of his girlfriend. In fact, both girls have been sent for, and Clitipho assures him that a whole procession will soon be arriving today: girls, servants, and the two slaves of the two households, whom the two young men have sent. Hence the 3rd pers. pl. of *cessant*.

illam Antiphila. Clitipho uses exaggerated language in 177 to suggest how silly Clinia's impatience is.

178-80 Chremes has been on stage, and in a short line he calls atten-tion to himself and starts the first conversation in the play between himself and his son. Clitipho notices him in 179 and pretends that it is a timely meeting. He gets to Clinia by ask-ing whether his father knows Menedemus, Clinia's father.

181-84 Clitipho quickly reveals that he is hosting Clinia, an old friend from childhood, whom he has brought home from the boat.

cenam a "welcome-home" dinner. Chremes is delighted to hear these facts, for plans suggest themselves to him.

185-87 He immediately wants to invite Menedemus over to join his son. (He knows that his neighbor regrets his harsh treatment of Clinia and longs for the chance to be reconciled with him.)

cave faxis regular Terentian Latin for *cave ne facias*

188-90   **quid se faciat** subjunctive of indirect question. "What he will do with himself." Terence uses *facere* idiomatically with an ablative and no preposition. Clitipho explains that Clinia has just arrived and is torn by fears of his father and his girl. Chremes fails to report that Clinia's father has changed. A lot of painful deception is going to follow from this.

191-92   Chremes pushes his way into the family situation. When he hears that Clinia is wretched (like his father), he ridicules his folly. Who could possibly be less wretched?

193-96   **reliqui** partitive gen. "What is left that he doesn't have?" A list of six good things occupies 194 to epitomize his good luck. But, Chremes adds, these all correspond to the attitude of their possessor.

    ditias contracted form of *divitias*

197-200   Clitipho defends Clinia in his worry about his father's anger. He was always harsh, and now especially he will cruelly take advantage of Clinia's weakness.

    plus satis supply *quam* between these two words. Chremes starts to query this judgment and presumably to tell Clitipho how mild Menedemus has become toward his son. But then he stops himself and in an aside to us asserts confidently that it is "useful" for Clinia to stay afraid of his father. Thus, Chremes adds to troubles, which he could dissolve. He will suffer for this. Clitipho has heard his father muttering and asks him what he said. Chremes puts him off by changing the subject. No matter what Chremes was like, Clinia should have endured it and stayed instead of going to Asia.

    mansum supply *esse*

201-3   In his inflexible conviction that fathers always must be obeyed, Chremes is subtly revealing how he regards his own son. He asks two rhetorical questions in 202 and 203, which betray his awkward bias. It was not a question of who would be dominant, but how two people could get along with real compromises and adaptations.

204-7   Now, Chremes invents excuses for his neighbor which deny his former harshness. Sententiously he produces a neat chiastic set of words at 206. But they are only promoting their bias. Talking in the 3rd pers. pl., Chremes does not realize where he stands with Clitipho, how he could help him toward virtue.

208-10 More preaching, all impersonally worded. The soul of a young man "chains" itself down by wicked desire—that's love, to the father—and the alliterative line 209 justifies the father's stern responses, now called *consilia*. This then is the reasonable conclusion: to draw from observation of others what might be useful for oneself. Clitipho will comment on this soon after his father leaves.

211-12 The son hardly "believes" what he has been told, so his answer is ironic. Chremes departs indoors to check on dinner, leaving Clitipho to an important soliloquy and reminding him to stay nearby. *sis = si vis.*

        Our text labels 213 ff. as Act II. However, there were originally no Acts in Roman comedies nor in the Greek plays they adapted. What is important now is the soliloquy of Clitipho.

213-15 Clitipho announces his theme in legal terms: fathers are unjust towards young men (e.g., sons). They think that after boyhood, males skip the stage of youth *(adulescentia)* and should be like old men, as their fathers are. They should have no contact with the normal things of youth.

216-19 "They rule (us) according to their present pleasure, not what formerly moved them." He goes on to declare that, if he ever has a son, he will be an easy-going father *(facilis,* not *durus).*

        ne here and at 222, the long vowel is shortened before the following vowel. The particle reinforces a positive statement. He will take time to recognize and forgive wrong. That will be different from his father, who uses others to give moral advice.

220-22 When Chremes has drunk a little too much, he regales his son with stories of his misdeeds (as *adulescens).* Thus, Chremes emerges as a moral hypocrite. Clitipho cites with disgust his father's words from 210. "Real smart" he labels Chremes.

223-24 He is more aroused by the demanding words of his prostitute girlfriend. But he is a victim of the tight ways of Chremes and has nothing to give his friend. Clearly, though the boy is full of self-pity, he reveals himself a fool for love.

225-26 By comparison, although Clinia has his own financial problems, too, still his Antiphila was brought up chastely, totally innocent of the mercenary and deceptive ways of a courtesan.

227-29 Clitipho lists five adjectives which epitomize the assertive, loud, and demanding personality of his Bacchis. When she asks for something, he says vaguely: "Sure," because it would be a sin to say he has no money: she would dump him. This is a new experience for him, and his father does not yet know about it.

230-31 **essent . . . venissent** subjunctives in contrary-to-fact clauses, present and past. Subject of the second verb is the women. Cf. the verb in 175. Clinia has recklessly come out of Clitipho's house to voice his worries. He fears that Antiphila has taken the courtesan's path in his absence.

232-34 "Many reasons come together to increase my feeling."

exaugeant subjunctive in consecutive clause after indefinite *multae opiniones*. Clinia now lists four items to back his suspicions. They contrast with the favorable list produced by Clitipho above in 226. The mother who ends the list strongly sounds like a woman who is manipulating her daughter toward prostitution, since money means so much to her and she "rules" Antiphila so harshly.

235-37 It is only now that Clitipho notices Clinia and warns him of his imprudence in showing himself outside the house.

mali partitive gen. with *nescioquid*. Clitipho tells him to stop prejudging the situation before he really knows its truth (cf. 237).

238-40 But they would have been here if there weren't some problem, says Clinia, and he ignores the reassurances of his friend. It's typical of women to take a year to get anything going (*esset, adessent,* contrary to fact).

241   When Clinia merely repeats his fears, Clitipho notices that some of the slaves are in sight, and tells Clinia to take a breath. The girls will soon arrive.

242-44 The meters since 175 have been conversational, mostly iambic variations. From here to the end of our passage at 256, Terence will use the trochaic septenarius, a popular musical meter. There will be four speakers now, the two young lovers and their respective slaves. Syrus belongs to Chremes and Clitipho; Dromo to Menedemus and Clinia. They are talking as they enter the stage, continuing what they said before their arrival.

sermones caedimus "cutting speech" is a fancy way of referring to their talk. The point is, they have stopped paying attention to the women they are leading to the house, and the women, no doubt immersed in some conversation, too, have lagged behind. However, Clitipho overhears enough to be able to reasssure Clinia that his girlfriend is approaching. And Clinia, who was sick with anxiety, now is cured. Through the next lines, the slaves continue to talk only to each other, unaware of the confusion they are causing their young masters. According to the conventions of dramatic presentation, they do not even see their masters.

245-46 Dromo notices that the women have lagged behind. No wonder, he says: they are so loaded down with baggage and extra servants. Here, we find Clinia totally confused and in despair because of what he understands of the situation. He knows that Antiphila has been sent for, but not that Bacchis is coming, too. He knows that he left Antiphila in deepest poverty, with a single servant (cf. 252 below). Where do these several servants come from?

illi Antiphila

247-50 Still talking about the women, Syrus says they shouldn't have been left behind. Understand a subject for *relictas* in *illas* and a completion of the infinitive with *esse*. When he comments on the mass of baggage they are bringing (actually, only Bacchis is), poor, deluded Clinia groans. Syrus adds to Clinia's misery by specifying gold and clothes in the baggage. Taking command, Syrus, a clever slave, notes the lateness of the day and dispatches Dromo to go meet the baggage train and the girls. Here, presumably, Dromo exited.

251-53 When his friend asks what's bothering Clinia at this point, he hears all the details of 252 and what they mean to Clinia. He has been fussing over these things since 245–46.

254-56 Meanwhile, the laggards approach. Syrus exclaims over the crowd of people. Moving to the future (254–55), he predicts a financial disaster for his master from the extravagant eating and drinking of these uninvited guests. We do not know yet that Syrus has some deception in mind: namely, that Baccchis will pose as Clinia's girlfriend and Antiphila will pose as a servant. This will really confuse the hypocritical Chremes and cost him money, and it will give Clitipho a chance to be with Bacchis for a while. He has just spotted his young masters (*eccos* 256) as the passage ends. Syrus is confident and carefree in the plan he has put together, while Clinia still needs to learn of the truly happy results of his return to Antiphila.

ᴄᴠ *PHORMIO, 161 BCE*

Plot Summary and Vigorous Ending

After the success in April of *Eunuch*, Terence and his public were primed for another comedy that same year. In September at the Roman Games, he successfully staged *Phormio*, choosing a simple name for the title instead of the long Greek participle which in the original defined Phormio's comic activity as *The Man Who Went to Law*. This is one of two Terentian plays that is adapted not from Menander, but from a young admirer named Apollodorus.

Plot Summary (12 lines)

Added to the manuscripts of all the comedies are plot summaries (or to use the Greek word, *periochae*) that were composed artfully in the second century CE by a man named C. Sulpicius Apollinaris. His art consisted in covering each of the plots in twelve lines of iambic senarii. As this example shows, Sulpicius concentrated on the bare details of the mixed-up relationships that form the basic structure of the plot. Demipho and Chremes are brothers, and each has a son, Antipho and Phaedria, ready for his first amatory experiences. Demipho leaves Athens and crosses the Aegean to Cilicia to claim an inheritance. The summary only mentions his leaving Athens. Chremes also leaves Athens for the island of Lemnos. The summary ignores this trip until line 609, but fills us in on Chremes' shabby treatment of his Athenian marriage. He was supposed to manage an estate of his wife on Lemnos, but instead, on his annual visits there, he has conducted a long affair with another woman, supporting her and their daughter who is now fourteen or fifteen. Thus, Chremes has two wives and two children, and his legitimate Athenian wife and son know nothing of his second household on Lemnos. But brother Demipho knows all and conspires against his own son and the wife and son of Chremes for the immoral convenience of his brother.

So far, I have greatly expanded the limited details Sulpicius offers in four and one-half lines. Most of that was background. Now, we move into the complications of the plot. First, the Lemnian mother sails to Athens because she is concerned for her marriageable daughter. Arriving in Athens, she dies, leaving her daughter alone in the strange city with a single servant. The daughter tends to her mother's funeral. Antipho spots her at this pathetic scene and falls in love at first sight of her beauty. The summary skips over a lot, merely reporting that, by the efforts of a parasite—that is Phormio—he gets the girl as his wife. That leaves out entirely the trickery of Phormio, who goes to law fraudulently and forces the servant to deliver the girl into Antipho's hands for marriage. Now, problems arise for the two cousins Antipho and Phaedria as they await the return of their angry fathers. But Terence will reverse our expectations and make fools of the much more guilty fathers.

We have reached line 9 of the summary. The fathers arrive utterly furious, "roaring," as Sulpicius nicely puts it.

9   **fremere** historical infinitive. They are angry at the marriage and Phormio's use of the law, but they soon realize that the wife of Antipho is Chremes' daughter, and they are caught in a bind. Before they discover the true identity of the wife, however, they bribe Phormio to take her off their hands and marry her himself. Phormio has figured out the embarrassing position of the fathers, so he has no intention of ruining Antipho's marriage. He takes the bribe money, which is enough to buy the freedom of the harpist beloved of Chremes' son (Phaedria), and so he engineers the erotic happiness of the second young man. There is an animated and angry confrontation between Phormio and the two fathers, the substance of the passage we are about to read, but ignored by the economic Sulpicius. So at the end of the comedy, the older men have been thoroughly frustrated and each of the young cousins has his beloved. For, as Sulpicius' last line reports, Antipho gets to keep his wife, now that the fathers recognize that she, as the daughter of Chremes' guilt, legitimizes the marriage.

Last Scenes of the Comedy (884–989): The Triumph of Phormio

884-87 Phormio enters on an empty stage. He has mastered all the lies that the fathers have told, and he intends to turn them to his own uses. Two opportunities have come his way simultaneously: first, he is going to fool the old men and, second, he is going to free Phaedria of money problems.

adimere Terence varies the gerund with an infinitive, each a similar verbal noun.

ne . . . supplex siet Phaedria will now have enough money so that he won't have to humililate himself all the time by begging for loans. Subjunctive in purpose clause describing Phormio's intention. This whole passage is in iambic senarii.

888-89 **ingratiis** Against the will of the fathers, Phormio has ex-
tracted thirty minae, and now he counts on giving the same
money also against the fathers' will to Phaedria for his love
affair. There is nothing they can do to resist him.

890-93 Phormio has of course been speaking to himself. Now, he announces to himself his conscious plans as actor. He is going
to change his movements and his facial expression from the
obsequious ones he used on the fathers to bilk them of their
money (*capiundus*: *capiendus*; *novos*: *novus*).

angiportum a side-alley or lane, regularly used in Roman
comedy as a place of hiding and secret observation. Phormio moves here in anticipation of the exit of the fathers from
Demipho's house. He wants to be able to choose the ideal moment for braving them. As he says, he had pretended that he
needed to do some shopping. But he jettisons that lie. (*adsimularam*: plpf., omitting -*ve*-).

hisce same suffix for "here" as in *Andria* 28 and 32

894-95 Demipho and Chremes enter in a mood of exultation and
thanksgiving identical to that of Phormio at 884. But they are
in for disappointment, justly so. They are happy over the fact
that Antipho's wife has proved to be Chremes' illegitimate
daughter, and now they can get back from Phormio the money
they reluctantly gave him as a bribe to marry that girl himself.

896-99 **conveniendust** gerundive with omission of *e* from *est*.

dilapidat "scatter wastefully like stones." This seems to be the
earliest use of this verb in Latin. Demipho talks anxiously of
"our" money, but Chremes has in fact put up every penny. As
soon as Phormio hears of their miserly anxiety, he seizes his
opportunity and saunters out from the alley, heading straight
for Demipho's house.

900-902 Phormio asks innocently but ironically whether they all have
the same reason for seeking each other. "Exactly," replies Demipho, greedily assuming that the whole issue is the money.

facerem subjunctive in double negative clause of fearing

903-5   Phormio puts on a fine act of injured honor, doubling *quanta* to stress his pathos.

      liberalis There is a tradition among some scholars to take this adjective as an insult against effeminacy in Phormio. But others, as I prefer, take it in the obvious sense of "real gentleman." In either case, the speaker is lying through his teeth, either with open hostility or false friendliness.

906-9   **nuntiatum** acc. of the supine. Phormio claims to be all ready for the marriage. With mock-seriousness, he asserts that he has put everything aside so as to gratify the brothers, since he saw how anxious they were.

      animum advorteram governs the infinitive of indirect discourse

910-12   Demipho now has to try his act of honor. Chremes, he alleges, has persuaded him that it is disgraceful to expel the girl once she has been married and bedded. So for a moment he plays the good man (until Phormio works some more on him).

913-14   Demipho even reminds Phormio of the moral arguments he used against driving the girl out of the house. They had no effect on the angry father at the time.

915-17   Phormio who is playing games with these men pretends that they are making a mockery of his honesty. He has burned all his bridges in his effort to speed up the marriage, including breaking off an engagement to marry another woman.

918-20   Chremes whispers to his brother another argument he could try, and Demipho speaks it word for word. But he quickly abandons that lie and resolves to commit himself to legal assistance.

921-22   **transi sodes** Demipho starts with an imperative verb (cf. *Andria* 85), then moderates his tone with the contracted form of *si audes* ("if you please"). We are supposed to know that it is a short distance from Demipho's house to "cross" to the forum or agora, where there are commercial agents who can reassign the thirty minae to Chremes.

923-24   **quodne** relative pronoun (referring to the silver) and the interrogative enclitic *ne*.

discripsi Phormio pretends that he has had to pay off a variety of acquaintances, from whom it will be hard to re-collect that money. He is acting innocent and outraged (and enjoying it).

924-29 Phormio goes through a routine of injured innocence. He puts it very simply: 1. If they want to go through with the arranged marriage, Phormio is here to take her. 2. If they want to change plans and keep the girl with them, fine. But the dowry which was to be paid to Phormio remains with him. It is not fair that he should lose money because of them. After all, for their sake he called off a marriage that he had arranged for himself, with a woman whose dowry had to be recovered (amazingly, the same amount of money).

930-32 Demipho does not want to give up those 30 minae, so he storms at Phormio in the hope of daunting him.

In' hinc malam rem the first word is colloquial *is* (from *ire* ["to go"], with the *s* compressed) + the interrogative sign *-n[e]*. The whole passage can be translated: "Will you go to Hell from here?"

magnificentia "big talk." Of course, both men are talking big, but we favor Phormio, who is not personally profiting from his tricks.

932-36 **irritor** "I am growing angry" or "I am being deliberately provoked." Demipho sneers his doubt that Phormio really would marry the girl he had taken in betrothal, and Phormio mocks back: "Just try me." Demipho tries out a false accusation, that Phormio is simply giving Antipho access to the girl. Then, the father comes back to his theme: hand over the money, which is answered in parody: hand over (*cedo*, imperative, cf. 950) the wife as agreed. Demipho plays then his last card: *in ius ambula*. This is the formula for demanding that a person with whom one is in disagreement must proceed to the court for an official ruling on the situation. That would frighten most lowly parasites, but Phormio still has his ace to play.

937-40 Phormio expands his counter-threat over several lines and while delaying some key details. He starts with an incomplete conditional sentence: "if you men are going to continue to be objectionable . . . ," which Demipho interrupts with a sneer: "What will you do?" The little question "I?" spoken with calm confidence, then moves us to a taunt by Phormio. "I suppose you think that I defend only women who have no dowry. I also protect dowered women."

patrocinari the verb takes the dative at 939 and is understood at 940. Chremes, who is affected by these ambiguous details, asks: What does that matter to us? Understand *refert* with the interrogative *quid id nostra*. Phormio's answer is a very blithe and cheerful: "oh nothing."

941-45 Phormio starts on his blackmail: "I knew a woman here whose husband . . . wife." There is a missing verb and some way of linking this wife with the husband that will prove highly embarrassing for Chremes. In the lacuna, the two brothers react differently. Chremes correctly guesses that his misdemeanor is exposed (exclamatory *hem*). Demipho acts puzzled, unable to construe this incomplete sentence. So Phormio completes the sentence in a surprising way. It turns out, as noted in my introduction and in the Periocha of Sulpicius, that the wife, for whom grammar is lacking in 941, is a rare victim of bigamy. In short clauses, while Chremes writhes in shame and fear, Phormio reports the birth of a daughter to the Lemnian couple (perfect tense) and then the raising of the child (present tense), to stress the fact that Chremes still continues his infidelity and his cheating of his Athenian wife by financing with her money for over a decade the costs of this daughter who is not hers. Chremes admits that he is "dead" and "buried." Next, Phormio says how he is protecting a dowered woman: he intends to tell her the whole story.

denarrabo The prefix helps to color Phormio's threat: he will enjoy his role as informer of Chremes' wife Nausistrata. Chremes weakly pleads with Phormio. Phormio acts surprised to have Chremes turn out to be the guilty unidentified husband of his story.

946-51 **missum te facimus** We release you from the charge we intended. Phormio knows that he is invulnerable, so he calls that mere fiction. When Chremes asks what he wants to be quiet, and offers as bribe the money they have been squabbling over, Phormio is in total control.

audio "I'm listening," he says, waiting for an apology and some human sense of shame. Then, to show us his power, he now proceeds to denounce the shilly-shallying of this pair of scoundrels and mocks them as guilty children, trying to avoid their blame.

952-56 **rescivit** Chremes asks his brother how Phormio found out all this damning detail. The verb is one that Terence uses to replace the Greek for *anagnorisis*. The person who "finds out" damning information about others (or himself) is by definition the central role of the comedy, because the information empowers him. Here, we see how Terence innovates and makes his "hero" a parasite, socially one of the lowest people of Athens. And yet Phormio has the power and right on his side and uses his information to emend the faulty qualities of this dysfunctional family.

957-63 Having no shame and nothing to lose, Demipho tries to be a hero and fight it out like a man with Phormio. He tells Chremes to act like a man with him. Since there is no way of stopping the ugly story from becoming public knowledge, what Chremes should do is beat Phormio to the gun and reveal his secret to his wife first.

tuom esse The hiatus—no elision—is marked by the line in the text.

elatum "brought out in the open." When she hears their story, maybe Nausistrata will be easier to reconcile. Note the double acc. (*id . . . uxorem*) with *celare*. At any rate, they will have stolen Phormio's advantage and can punish him later. This is neither very manly nor heroic, but it seems quite consistent with the truculent nature of Demipho.

inpuratum The epithet is biased and hypocritical, not in the least corresponding to the character of Phormio who has been debonairly performing for us. But Phormio in 963 is not resting on his oars: he guesses the strategy of the evil pair. Hence *atat*.

964–67 These brothers may talk of being manly, but Phormio mocks the bellicose or gladiatorial spirit they have mustered. Chremes is already doubting the success of their approach to Nausistrata.

vereor ut placari possit clause of fearing in the negative sense. "I'm afraid that she can't be appeased." Demipho tries to encourage Chremes, by reminding him that his Lemnian wife is now dead and cannot cause trouble, even though her daughter is very much alive and in Athens.

968–75 Phormio verbally attacks the brothers in a strident, righteous manner, further acting out his moral superiority. The action of the three is approximately as follows. When Phormio said he would denounce Chremes to Nausistrata, he moved towards the house of Nausistrata. But when Demipho urged a counter-attack by anticipating Phormio's information, the brothers moved over to intercept and anticipate Phormio. This is, then, a mock-battle.

971 **veritus feminae** This verb can take the genitive in Archaic Latin.

972 **novo modo** Phormio may well be referring to the novel misdeed of Chremes practicing bigamy. Not that it was totally novel, but it was outrageous.

lautum accusative of the supine with verb of motion (*venias*)

974–75 Phormio borrows from a fire metaphor to emphasize the effect of his report on Nausistrata, who will blaze up with anger, a fire that cannot be put out by Chremes' torrent of tears.

976–81 **malum quod** Demipho jumps into the exchange of threats, praying that the "evil" predicted by Phormio ought to fall on him, not Chremes.

duint archaic optative form of *dare*: "may the gods give"

hoc . . . scelus "this crime" = "this criminal." (*asportarier* archaic pres. pass. for *-ari*). Terence facilitates the meter at the end of the line by adding a final syllable. Phormio should be punished, according to Demipho, who has no sense of shame for what he and Chremes have done. Chremes is ashamed and worried, but does not know what to do against Phormio. But Demipho quickly declares he knows: resort to law, where he has some chance of influencing the outcome. He summons Phormio according to the regular formulae. But Phormio confidently answers him. Instead of trooping over to the agora for official treatment, he points to a different destination ("over here," *huc*), meaning the door of Nausistrata's house. She will decide the issue, in the light of her own interests.

982-86   Terence works out a scene of quite funny action here, as he shows the feeble and guilty older brothers trying to take on the athletic and mocking Phormio as each side cries out for Nausistrata's powerful attention. Weak-willed Chremes asks his brother to take on the battle, while he will go indoors to call for some help from the slaves. Demipho tells him to hurry, because he is not strong enough to handle Phormio alone. Apparently, Demipho hits Phormio. Meanwhile Chremes hits him from the other side. It is a comic free-for-all, when Phormio plays his winner: I don't need to beat you two up—I shall use my voice against you: *voce* 985; *opus est* with ablative.

986-89   As Phormio uses his voice to call Nausistrata to the door, Chremes tells his brother to stop up that filthy mouth. Phormio dismisses the command with surprise and defiance. The two brothers are hitting their quarry and tugging him away from the house, and Demipho urges feeble Chremes to smash Phormio in the stomach if he refuses to move away with them. We can see that Phormio has put himself in the dominant position, moral and actual, as he calls Chremes' wife out. The final 70 lines of the comedy show Nausistrata assuming the authority over Chremes in her household and declaring that the *iudex* hereafter will not be the father but she and her son

Phaedria. For his reward, Phormio gets an invitation to dinner (true to the desires of a parasite) and the pleasure of eating
to his heart's delight in front of the shamed Chremes.

∾ HECYRA, *Written 164 BCE, Finally Staged to the End 160*

Misunderstandings

The Greek title *Hecyra* is translated as *The Mother-in-Law*. This is
a play that gave Terence much anguish, because it was performed
in 164, Spring 160, and September 160, and only on the final occasion did the actors complete their performance. Earlier, it failed to
compete with other entertainment of the festal occasion, and so it
lost its audience and closed down. Terence planned it as a worthy
successor to *Andria*, developing what we would call a feminist touch.
His play's mother-in-law is not the typical mother-in-law of comedy
and popular stories, not a despot in the house and harsh ruler of her
daughter-in-law, but she is victimized by the stereotype.

Our passage comes from the second scene. The first scene, as is
the way in Terence, gives some background to the play, and, as Terence liked to do, it gives a confident but mistaken account of the situation. There are two families living next door: two fathers, Laches
and Phidippus; their wives, Sostrata and Myrrina; their children,
respectively the son of Laches and Sostrata named Pamphilus and
the daughter of the other couple, Philumena. These children have
grown up, and their parents have arranged for their marriage several
months ago. There are some servants and slaves, too, but the only
slave who plays an important role is Parmeno; and he has no part in
the passage we are treating.

It is customary, if the husband's mother is alive and well, for the
newly married to move in with his parents, and for the daughter-in-
law to try to adapt herself to the ways of the elderly mother. There
was no open indication of disagreement in the first months of this
marriage. Nevertheless, no sooner had Pamphilus left Athens to
check on an inheritance than Philumena also left the house, without
explanation, and returned to her own parents' house. The natural

explanation of this mysterious move was to blame it all on the mother-in-law Sostrata. Efforts to call on the girl's parents and to clear up
the problem have totally failed. The slave Parmeno, who supplies the
inaccurate background information, goes along with the standard reaction: that Sostrata has behaved like a typical mother-in-law, and her
nastiness has compelled Philumena to flee back home. Our passage
deals with the upset household of Sostrata, her plainly mild manners,
and the irascible and typical accusations of her husband Laches. Meter is variety of iambic septenarii and octonarii, long lines.

198-204 Terence starts with a scene of marital misunderstanding out-
        side the home of Laches and Sostrata, parents of Pamphilus
        and in-laws of Philumena. Laches storms on stage from the
        house (where we can assume their conversation started), and
        Sostrata follows him, timid and worried. Laches starts off
        with exclamations against the female sex and what he calls
        their conspiracy (*utin*: exclamatory interrogative). All women
        are the same in what they want and don't want!

200   **reperias** Laches addresses the air and inevitably the audience,
        not Sostrata. Hence, the subjunctive. Now we come to the prej-
        udicial generalization: all mothers-in-law hate their daughters-
        in-law. In addition, they all are eager to oppose their husbands,
        so that to this husband all women have been trained alike in
        the same school to spite their mates. If there is any such school
        (and of course there isn't), Sostrata is the ideal teacher.

205-10 In contrast to her loudly assertive husband, Sostrata's meek
        protests tend to win our favor. She characterizes herself as
        miseram, a victim of unfair accusation, and she protests that
        she doesn't know the reason. Laches immediately takes her
        up on the claim to be ignorant. She invokes the gods and her
        hope that she and Laches continue to live together. But in his
        fury he claims not to share her hope. She then predicts that
        he will eventually realize (*rescisces*, 208) that she was unjust-
        ly accused (cf. *Phormio* 952). That Latin verb often appears
        at the moment of discovery in Terence, where the plot and

characters are at last correctly revealed. (In this play, Sostrata receives no such recognition from Laches.)

211-16 Laches predicts that their in-law neighbors will turn from friends to enemies, that they will regret choosing Pamphilus for their daughter. He has been suspicious for a long time of Sostrata and had her spied on. It turns out that they have a convenient marital arrangement: Sostrata, who likes to be near her woman friends, lives in Athens, while he spends most of his time watching over the farm several miles away in the countryside. But he resents her pleasure in the city and keeps himself informed of the things that she and the maids do in his absence (*vestrarum* "you women" cf. 240).

217-22 Already he has heard and believed the rumor that Philumena has started to hate her mother-in-law. It is a typical situation, not surprising (*mage* 220 = *magis*). But this is worse: Laches believes that his daughter-in-law hates the entire household. If he had known that, then he would have insisted on her staying in the house and Sostrata leaving her home.

223-29 **immerito** Laches stresses his innocence as Sostrata had in 208. All this has been her fault, he asserts, and he can't figure out how to cure this sickness (*aegritudo*). He deserves better from her after all his sacrifices. As he views their arrangement, he was the one who paid. He left Athens and went to the farm for her sake, to tend to the family finances and see to it that she lived in comfort while he slaved on the farm, all contrary to what a man of his age should expect.

230-34 **curares** subjunctive expressing obligation. While Laches was toiling on the farm, he expected his wife to see that everything went smoothly in Athens, especially since he had freed her from other domestic duties. As he sees things, she should be ashamed at her age of starting a war against a young girl. He can hardly imagine that she will claim that it was the girl's fault (232). And she doesn't before he presses on. He is glad for his son's sake that she does not accuse Philumena. In her case, though, Sostrata in doing wrong has gone to the limit of fault.

235–42 Sostrata mildly proposes a possible alternate explanation: had the girl pretended this hatred, to create an excuse for visiting her mother longer? Laches has a quick answer: when Sostrata went to the girl's house to ask after her, nobody allowed her in. That was a likely sign of real enmity. She replies that the servants in the house said she was simply exhausted and needed to rest. That was the reason that she was not admitted. It was your behavior that caused the girl's "sickness" (*morbum*, 239), he rejoins. This is the most particular explanation yet of what went wrong with the girl. Nobody can figure it out. Scholars long ago noted that the original Greek play would have provided an explanation in the opening section, for us in the audience. But Terence planned a more devious and lengthy approach to the truth. I shall respect his plot and postpone revelation until the end of this selection, at 280.

243–50 Things are at an impasse between Laches and Sostrata, but he has voiced deep suspicions. So far, we have not seen in the play anyone from the bride's house. Now, her father emerges, the least likely to control any reliable information. Phidippus is another Laches. As he comes out, he finishes up an argument that he was having with Philumena. He wants her to go back to her mother-in-law, and she does not want to.

250 **heia vero** Phidippus protests against Laches' claim.

251–57 Laches has tried to call on Phidippus at home yesterday, but was sent away (*amisi*, contracted form of *amisisti*) without an answer. That isn't right, argues Laches, to conceal one's anger when you are supposedly creating a strong union by marriage between two families. Rather, if we have done something wrong, tell us so that we can fix the problem to your satisfaction, either by showing you your error or by clearing ourselves by apologies. If, however, you are keeping the girl home because she is sick, you are doing wrong to distrust us and be afraid that she would not be most carefully cared for in Laches' house.

257   **metuis ... ut ... curetur** subjunctive in a negative clause of
      fearing, with the conjunction *ut*

258-66 Laches insists that he has a strong feeling for Philumena, to
      rival Phidippus' love. And he particularly recognizes the love
      of Pamphilus, who, he is sure, loves her as much as he does
      himself and will take it very hard if he learns (*rescierit*, 262).
      Laches is therefore eager that she return to his house before
      Pamphilus returns from his trip. *studeo* takes a final clause
      with or without *ut* and also an infinitive clause (cf. 265). What
      can the embarrassed Phidippus answer?

267-73 Laches also asks whether Philumena has some complaint
      against Pamphilus. Not at all, says Phidippus, and he goes on
      to cite the girl's way of opposing his pressure on her to return
      to her in-laws. She swore that she could not endure being in
      the house as long as Pamphilus was absent. That suggests of
      course that Sostrata is the problem for her. Delicately, though,
      Phidippus blames himself. Various people have various faults.
      His particular weakness is his gentle temper: he can't bring
      himself to oppose members of his family. The men leave the
      stage for the forum (273).

274-80 Sostrata's short soliloquy ends this scene. Against the mass of
      prejudice that the men have voiced, it stands as a convincing
      statement of her innocence and ignorance. She blames a few ex-
      ceptional women for this negative typology. It is hard to break
      this type and to exculpate herself. Men are too quick to blame
      all women. Sostrata knows she does not fit the type (*mequidem*
      subjunctive of another indirect statement, which denies that
      she copies all other mothers-in-law). She has consistently treat-
      ed this daughter-in-law as a beloved member of the family. She
      still does not know how this disaster has happened to her.

279   **Qui ... eveniat** subjunctive of indirect question (*qui* = later
      abl. *quo*). Her last line, looking forward to the return of Pam-
      philus, functions as a transition to the next scene, when, af-
      ter Sostrata goes into her home, Pamphilus does appear. He

learns from Parmeno a garbled version of affairs, but soon finds out for himself that Philumena has a special kind of "sickness": she is in her last minutes of pregnancy, about to give birth. This fact absolves Sostrata of blame, but it immediately demands the explanation of her pregnancy, which becomes a major problem for Pamphilus and the household of Philumena. The recognition is far off.

✆ Terence's EUNUCH, 161 BCE, His Most Successful Play

Characterization

Each of Terence's six plays contains at the start of some manuscripts short information that bears on the occasion of the first performance. I have chosen the editorial data (*Didascalia*) for *Eunuch* as an example of this information. First, we learn the name of the comedy. Next, we learn of the festival on which it was produced and the two curule aediles who authorized and paid for the performance as their public responsibility. Then, the two men who managed the actors and staged the play are listed. Ambivius managed all six of Terence's comedies and some of his predecessor's Caecilius'; Atilius from Praeneste coproduced several. As part of the staging, we are next told of the flute player Flaccus who accompanied the poetic verse with a pair of flutes. Then, Greek Menander appears as the source of Terence's Latin version and its Greek title. In the collection familiar to this editor, *Eunuch* was Terence's second play. (Modern scholars consider it rather the third or fourth comedy.) And finally, the first staging of this play is dated to the consulship of Valerius and Fannius, which was 161 BCE.

The plot and title of this comedy focus on the immature ephebe Chaerea, who spots a beautiful girl on the streets of Athens and passionately pursues her and heedlessly rapes her in her house. He gets into the house disguised as a eunuch, a supposedly valuable gift for the girl's mistress. Rapes are common in Greek and Latin comedies, because they so dramatically disrupt family plans, but are capable of surprisingly happy reconciliations. Nevertheless, Chaerea's rape of the innocent girl is meant to shock us, and I have chosen his narrative of the episode that reveals him as a moral eunuch, not the smart trickster that he seems to think he is. The meter is a mixture of various long iambic measures punctuated by an occasional trochaic septenarius.

539-41   We know that Terence modified his Menandrian source here. Menander had Chaerea perform a rhapsodic soliloquy when he came out from the house after his sneaky rape. Terence, on the contrary, created the role for Antipho so that he could share the rapist's exultation over his clever coup and so that Chaerea could consciously act out self-congratulation before a friend as well as before us. Terence accounts for Antipho by inventing a dinner that Chaerea is supposed to be organizing, which Antipho is checking on because of the mysterious absence of his friend.

coiimus "we arranged together"

in Piraeo The Piraeus was the port city of Athens.

540   **in hunc diem** "for today"

de symbolis The friends promised to contribute specific foods to the dinner.

essemus impf., subjunctive from *edere*, "to eat"

541   **praefecimus** "We put Chaerea in charge." Chaerea's neglect of his agreement and duty to his friends is one additional mark of his selfish immaturity.

dati anuli The rings were like an IOU, guaranteeing to pay for the promised contributions. These quick short phrases are typical of Terence's narrative style.

542   **quo in loco dictumst** i.e., *in eo loco quo cenare dictumst*, "in the place where we agreed to dine"

nil est parati gen. of whole. No trace of preparations can be detected.

543-44 Antipho has looked all over the Piraeus for Chaerea, with no success. Now the others in the planned dinner have sent him back to Athens to find his friend.

545-48 Antipho's arrival coincides with the emergence of Chaerea from the house next door, which belongs to Thais. He is dressed in the clothes of the eunuch which he borrowed; and he looks very odd. Antipho's reaction is a series of amazed questions and exclamations (*hominist* gen. *malist*, cf. 546) as he hesitates to recognize Chaerea in this disguise and wonders why he is emerging from a neighboring house, not from his own. To play it safe, Antipho stops and watches from a distance what his friend does. So he overhears Chaerea's entrance-speech before stepping forward in 557 and making contact with him.

549 A favorite comic situation. Chaerea asks himself whether anyone else is on stage, either before or behind him, and he proceeds to some clownish movements of search, but fails to identify the person we can clearly see there.

550-52 **erumpere** Normally intransitive, the verb is used transitively here. Knowing that he has not acted responsibly in the rape, Chaerea wants to make sure it is safe to let his pleasure erupt. His appeal to Jupiter attests his extreme passion. In a mood where his sexual success is so special, like more conventional lovers, i.e., Tristan and Isolde, Chaerea prates of accepting death at this moment rather than risk having his joy spoiled by the passing moment.

vita nom. subject

553-56 Chaerea is disappointed that he has no rapt audience, for he still does not see Antipho.

neminemne . . . intervenire exclamatory infinitive clause. "What! No nosy person butting in."

qui me sequatur potential subjunctive, along with the two final verbs of 554

rogitando the verb of asking, on which the indirect questions of 555–56 depend. The verb is a gerund, abl. of means. Chaerea pretends that his expected audience would annoy him, but in fact he is bursting with the news of his exploit (*siem* archaic for *sim* of 566).

557–59   **adibo** Antipho at last announces that he will end this series of apparent monologues and make contact with his friend.

gratiam Antipho recognizes that Chaerea, in spite of his words, will consider it a favor to be asked eagerly to narrate his story. He parrots the questions of Chaerea, with an irony that prepares for us to enjoy the situation.

560–62   **quid taces?** For a moment, Chaerea is silent, and to our amusement and his, Antipho points this out. Chaerea then releases a torrent of enthusiastic words. This presumably is the suture that Terence creates in combining the character Antipho, whom he has invented for this dialogue situation, with the monologue of Chaerea in Menander's comedy.

o festus dies hominis It is not clear whether Chaerea means this is a festival day or that he considers Antipho a veritable festival.

cuperem potential subjunctive

narra Antipho asks for the narration, which impatient Chaerea quickly gratifies.

563–64   In the earlier part of the play, Terence introduced Chaerea's brother Phaedria and his difficult love for his neighbor Thais, who earns her living as a courtesan. Phaedria is set up as a contrast to his younger brother, weak but at least respectful of social propriety. Chaerea then narrates what the audience knows is false. He assumes that the girl he has seen entering Thais' house is a gift who will be prostituted by Thais. We have been told that in fact Thais regards the girl as her "sister" and is trying to find her original family in Athens to gain her freedom and social respectability. Chaerea assumes that he can presume on the rights of Thais and the girl's innocence.

565-66 **praedicem** deliberative subjunctive

siem = *sim* Terence borrows the archaism as often for metrical reasons (cf. *Phormio* 635, *sies* for *sis*; Hecyra 509, *siet* for *sit*; *Heauton Timoroumenos* 221, 237, and 252).

noris syncopated form of *noveris*. Knowing what a particular student of female beauty Chaerea is, Antipho should be able to infer the beauty of the girl from his enthusiasm.

567-68 When Chaerea says that he was overwhelmed by the girl's beauty, Antipho's response is undoubtedly ironic. After all, Chaerea has only seen this girl being escorted down the street. from some distance.

primam "first-rate"

amare coepi It is obvious how trivialized the idea of love is in this ephebe. But it is even worse when we see how far he will proceed on his "love."

569-71 Here, we catch up on some more narrative detail that Terence had already introduced to his audience. Phaedria, Chaerea's brother has been trying to buy the favors of Thais, so he had recently got for her a eunuch-slave as a present. It is obvious how useful it would be having a eunuch to protect the household of females. Turkish harems were notorious for their eunuchs. It is equally clear that a fully-equipped male disguised as a eunuch could wreak havoc in a harem or in Thais' trusting home. Phaedria had left instructions that their household slave Parmeno should deliver the real eunuch to Thais' house.

submonuit Parmeno, a typical clever slave, suggested an idea to Chaerea, which he immediately seized upon.

571-72 **quid id est?** Antipho asks what is the idea of Parmeno, and Chaerea spells it out in detail: to exchange clothes with the eunuch, and then have himself taken into Thais' house as though a eunuch, the perfect present for Thais.

ducier archaic for *duci*; Terence gets an extra syllable for his meter

573　Antipho still does not grasp the point, so he asks the question that stirs in some of the slower members of the audience: What advantage does Chaerea seek?

caperes subjunctive of purpose

574-77　**viderem** three successive purpose subjunctives outline Chaerea's vague intention to be with the gorgeous girl whom he claims to love. After asking for Antipho's approval of this reasoning, he continues with his narrative. In his eunuch-disguise, he was delivered to Thais, who gladly accepted the gift, took him indoors, and immediately assigned him to take care of the girl. Exactly what Chaerea could want, and the last thing the girl needs! Antipho's questions reflect the audience's.

satis tuto tamen? *tuto* is the adverb. "Was it safe?"

578-80　Thais gives strict instructions about keeping men away from the girl and closely attending her. They are to stay out of sight of strangers deep in the house.

modeste Chaerea acts out his role as obedient slave-eunuch, and Antipho comments on his hypocrisy: *miser.* Thais ends her speech by announcing that she is due to go to dinner (with a soldier-rival of Phaedria).

581-82　For the next 17 lines, the narration is uninterrupted. That might indicate that Terence is following more closely the original text of Menander, a monologue. A distinction is made between the trusted servants who attend Thais to her dinner and, on the other hand, a few *noviciae puellae*, girls recently acquired by Thais and still in training. All indicates that Thais runs a house of prostitution.

adornant They simply get the girl ready to bathe, because they have to take her clothes off, obviously.

583-85　Chaerea continues to act his role as a zealous eunuch, telling the other girls to hurry (*properent: indirect command*). The girl waits in a small room and studies a wall-painting, which shows an erotic scene from Greek myth, such as have been excavated at bordellos in Pompeii, but also in ordinary homes. This painting is the earliest example of *ekphrasis* in Latin literature (though it probably derives from Menander and therefore is Greek in origin). In *ekphrasis*, a picture or artistic object is described, and a relationship is indicated between the painting and the dramatic situation of the play. The painting depicts the arrival of Jupiter in a shower of gold to Danae, who was being fiercely guarded by her father Acrisius. The shower entered Danae (*gremium*), and in due time she became mother of Perseus, destined for many heroic ventures.

586-89 The girl is looking at a picture, where Danae suffers a rape too. But the girl has no reason to suspect the resemblance yet. On the other hand, when Chaerea starts to look at the picture, he immediately sees the likeness between himself and Jupiter the rapist. He is fired to perpetrate the rape by the scene of the god's arrival in Danae's house (*inpendio* 587 abl. of measure, "by a great deal," "greatly"). Forcing the resemblance, Chaerea ignores the golden shower and argues that the god had disguised himself as a man (as Chaerea poses as a eunuch) and secretly gained entry to the house of Acrisius (as he to Thais' home). He forgets entirely that he should be playing the role of guardian, not rapist. Literally, according to Chaerea's reading of the painting, the god gains entry by climbing in through the roof, by way of the impluvium, the opening over the atrium, through which rain water drained into an open pool.

fucum factum mulieri "to play a trick on the woman." The verb *factum* is acc. of the supine.

590-91 Chaerea exclaims over the power of Jupiter, to whom he compares himself.

non facerem "I a mere man, was I not to do what Jupiter did?" Deliberative subjunctive.

ita feci Momentarily, Chaerea jumps ahead of his narrative to report how willingly he did the rape.

592-93 While he is staring thoughtfully at the picture, the other girls come to take the beauty off to her bath (*lavatum*, acc. of supine).

With three successive verbs at the start of 593, Chaerea quickly gets closer to his point: She went, she bathed, she came back. The servant-girls make her comfortable on a bed, to nap after her bath and to await them, who will now bathe.

594-96 Chaerea continues to play his humble slave role, waiting for orders. Now, he is addressed by the eunuch's name and handed a little fan and told to make a light breeze for the girl. He is promised that he can bathe after the servant girls if he wants to.

facito, lavato fut. imperative. He pretends to be unhappy with this task, concealing the fact from the servants, but not from Antipho, that everything has worked out to put the girl in his clutches.

597-98 Antipho, as we near the climax of the narration, interrupts for the first time since 580. He clearly underlines the dishonesty of Chaerea's *tristis*, mocking his impudent face, posing with the fan, and behaving like a stupid donkey. Donkeys were proverbial for stupidity and stubbornness. They were also thought to be over-sexed, which is not inappropriate here. Cf. Apuleius'novel about the golden ass.

599-600 We left the servant giving him orders in 596. Chaerea continues from that point of the narrative. The girls rush off to the bath and make lots of girlish noise, as happens when slaves are temporarily free of their masters' presence. Chaerea is building up the suspense—*proruont* for active *proruunt*.

601-3 All conditions provide welcome comfort for the girl after her bath, and she falls asleep. Chaerea (Dorus) is fanning the sleeping girl, and looking at her from the side, where he is posted, he assures himself of her total vulnerability.

limis i.e., *oculis*. This side glance often implies a sneaky purpose, as here. Having peeked through the fan at the girl, Chaerea now checks the room and probably the happy noises of the bathing servants, to make sure the coast is clear *sati(s)n(e) . . . sint*, indirect question. Totally "free" to follow his "love" (lust), he then places the bar in the door to lock it tight.

604-6   Antipho serves as the unimaginative audience, waiting for the
climax of the narrative. But Terence neatly avoids all account
of the rape itself, leaving it to us to react to the egotistic account
of Chaerea. He indignantly responds to Antipho's question,
calling him "stupid" and then gets him to agree this was a god-
given opportunity that he could not afford to lose. The procession of adjectives and participial adjectives about this precious
moment turn the rape from the ugly thing it really was into a
golden opportunity only a fool would reject. Such a fool would
indeed be the very eunuch he was pretending to be.

essem contrary-to-fact subjunctive

607-8   Antipho tamely accepts the narrative and agrees with Chaerea about the rape, it seems. Instead, he brings up the subject of the friends' dinner that accounts for his role in this
play. And Chaerea, having implied the success of his "love,"
drops the subject, too, and plunges into dinner preparations.
It should be noted, however, that this is the only rape in New
Comedy, Greek or Latin, where the rapist acts soberly and in
the daytime. Chaerea, it now appears, did his job of getting
the dinner ready, and Antipho congratulates him and only
needs to ask where they will dine. At Chaerea's home? No,
not a good idea, obviously.

609-11   Antipho registers a mild objection that the dinner-site at Discus's house is too far away, and Chaerea acts as though he
chose the spot before the rape. He needs to change his eunuch
clothes and turn back into a respectable ephebe. But he can't
enter his house and change.

domo exsulo nunc Chaerea uses a metaphorical verb, which
rings morally truer than he suspects. He is an "exile" now because he has raped a freeborn friend of Thais and also fouled
up his relationship with his brother Phaedria. Through most
of the remainder of the comedy, Chaerea is stuck in the cos-
tume of the eunuch, epitomizing his real disgrace.

612-14   The two young men head for Antipho's house, to find some
clothes for Chaerea. Their last words, as they leave the empty

stage, concern the rape victim. Chaerea wants to figure out with his buddy a plan to get possession of the poor girl (whom he thinks a slave that he can acquire somehow). The rapist has further plans.

✂ *Adelphoe, 160 bce, Last Play, Prologue and Ending*

The Prologue of *The Brothers*

We know that Terence produced this comedy at his friend Scipio's own expense, as a part of the public funeral of his father, Aemilius Paulus, victor over the Macedonians at Pydna. The comedy and more popular sports like gladiatorial combats and acrobatic feats were customary ways of celebrating at his death a major political figure by his ambitious family. Nothing in the play refers to this occasion: the play is everything. It was customary to start a play with a prologue, written by the playwright, but spoken by the producer or an anonymous member of the cast, to introduce the audience to the drama. Plautus regularly does this; Terence does so in all six comedies. But the two poets vary on their methods. Plautus warms the audience up with jokes, witty comments on the fiction of a Greek play in Rome, and he also gives background details that enable him to plunge into the comedy in Act I. Terence is very serious, bent on dealing with his critics beforehand and his writing of this play. You would think that the death of the old hero Paulus was much more important and the process of luring the audience to take an interest in the plot of the play, but Terence seems focused on his own problems. He uses the discursive meter, a very polished iambic senarius.

1   **poeta** The speaker of this prologue is referring to Terence in the 3rd person (although Terence has written about himself for this speaker). Note the alliteration of *p* and *s* in this first line.

2   **scripturam** The script of the play has been leaked out to some of Terence's rivals. That implies that the play had been written well before Aemilius' death.

ad<u>vo</u>rsarios In 160 BCE, this use of *-vor-* was normal, but the change to Classical *-ver-* gradually took effect, according to Quintilian in the second century BCE. There is no difference in the two groups named in 2.

3 **rapere in peiorem partem** "grabbed for damage"

quam i.e., *scripturam*

4 **indicio** dative of purpose. Terence starts the metaphor of the courtroom, talking of himself as both defendant and witness. This line is a near-perfect chiasmus, which suggests how carefully Terence words his "defense."

5 **laudin an vitio** predicative datives as alternatives. The subjunctive is an indirect question, started with *n(e) an* and depending on the verbal force of judging in *iudices*.

6 **Synapothnescontes Diphili** Diphilus was a very popular Greek comic poet, perhaps twenty years older than Menander. Plautus mentions him, too. The Greek title of his comedy here may be translated as "Dying Together" (as in Plautus' title). We don't have the Greek, so we cannot reliably conjecture how the scene referred to in 8–9 functioned.

9-11 Diphilus had early in his play a common situation, in which a young lover, presumably short of funds to buy his beloved, simply kidnapped her from the pimp who owned her. Plautus dropped that scene, but Terence picked it up and translated it, supposedly word for word, for his *Brothers*.

12-14 Terence has admitted plagiarism, but now he proceeds to justify himself. The choice of explanations is simple robbery (that is, deliberate plagiarism) or the rescue (*reprehensum*) and purposeful use of a situation that had been wrongly neglected by Plautus. Terence had rescued it!

15-16 **nam** This starts a second response to Terence's critics, whom he brands as "malicious." The comedy is, as I said, produced by Scipio Aemilianus. The critics are sneering that Terence's political friends are writing, or helping to write, the comedies. This is probably a less serious charge than that of plagiary.

17-21   Terence devotes a single line (17) to the killing charge that
his enemies wrongly think they have launched, but four lines
to his artful response. He converts their *maledictum* into supreme praise, for himself and for his supporters. I am glad to
be known as having such distinguished friends, he seems to
say, who have benefited the state in war and peace and helped
others generously in private needs.

22-25   Here, Terence expressly notes he has left out what is conven-
tionally a part of every prologue: the *argumentum* or background to the plot, which helps to situate the audience in the
play as it starts. He claims that the two old men who open
the comedy will remedy the omission. They will both speak
part of the background and reveal the rest in the course of
acting their roles through to the end. So the *argumentum* has
been shifted to other portions of the comedy, not lost. It is
now clear that whatever prologue Menander wrote for his
original has been totally changed and reorganized by Terence.
He therefore ends by asking the audience for a fair hearing
(*aequanimitas vestra*).

25   **augeat** This implies that the poet expects to write more. Un-
fortunately, this is his last play.

The Ending of *The Brothers*

The actual background to this play is made puzzling by the decision
of Terence to add the scene omitted by Plautus and to forgo the tra-
ditional information of the Prologue. I here supply an *argumentum*.
There are two pairs of brothers, Micio the bachelor and Demea the
father of another pair of brothers, Aeschinus and Ctesipho. Micio
has adopted the elder son, Aeschinus, with the provision that Demea
would not interfere with his way of bringing up the boy. That proves
too difficult for strict Demea, because Micio is remarkably permissive and kind to Aeschinus. The opening of the play lets the two
fathers argue over the merits of strict and permissive upbringing,
and Demea goes away angry, because he enters with the report that
Aeschinus has stormed into a pimp's house and kidnapped one of his

girls after raining down blows on the pimp. Here is where the scene from Diphilus enters into use. But there is an important distinction. In Diphilus, the assailant was a young man in love with the girl; Demea assumes the same amatory relation for Aeschinus, but that is an error. He is helping brother Ctesipho in his affair with the girl, and Demea draws the wrong conclusion from ignorance. We know no better, for lack of information in the Prologue. The two older brothers are misled by the familiar situation, and so we agree with Demea that Aeschinus has been brought up as a spoiled brat, and we tend to consider Ctesipho a model of strict upbringing.

Eventually, all but temperamental Demea work out the truth, much to Micio's relief. However, no sooner has Aeschinus been redeemed than it turns out that he has raped the neighbor's daughter and, while dilly-dallying, nine months have nearly passed.

She is to have her baby (without a father and husband), and Aeschinus has simply avoided the issue until it is just about too late. Demea does not know about this but soon learns and accuses his brother once more of foolish liberality.

Demea, however, is more foolish, because he does not know how deeply Ctesipho is involved in his love affair, nor how much help he is getting from Micio. Terence therefore develops his comic plot along two lines: (1) He shows the whole household of Micio cheerfully united in undoing the tolerable errors of Aeschinus, in protecting Ctesipho from his father, and enjoying making a fool of Demea every time he angrily enters; (2) Demea is alone in criticism of Micio's permissiveness and always ignorant of the current situation. Only at the end of the comedy does he make an adjustment that brings these two plot lines into better balance. That is where we start.

787-90   Demea has been on stage with Syrus, and chanced to discover that Micio has taken Ctesipho into his home. Erupting in anger, he has forced his way past the door to find out more, and Syrus has decided prudently to take a nap in a corner. That leaves the stage briefly empty. Then Micio comes out of Sostrata's house calmly, and about the same time Demea rushes out of Micio's house in a state of totally wild despair.

Micio is concentrating on preparations to bring Aeschinus' beloved and baby over to her new home; Demea is focused on what has happened to his son Ctesipho. Thus, when the two brothers encounter each other, they talk at cross-purposes. Micio cannot even finish his words to Sostrata in 788 before the loud banging of doors inside his house stops him.

789   **quid faciam?** The series of exclamatory questions convey Demea's feelings of helplessness either to act or speak. In 790, he dramatizes that by calling on the three natural forces felt by mankind: heaven, earth, and ocean. The editor has put that sequence in quotes, because the language is atypical for Demea amd similar to the tragic effusions that have survived to us from the Latin tragedies popularly performed in Terence's day.

790-94   **em tibi** "That's your problem," Micio says to himself, realizing only too well what has happened.

791   **rescivit omnem rem** This is the moment of tragic or comic discovery and realization. Comic realization can usually be turned toward a happy ending, whereas tragic discovery regularly involves a death and its sadness. Notice how unsympathetic Micio appears. He registers the shouting of Demea, but does not respond to it except with an impatient *ilicet*. More fighting, where he must take his role in the defense.

793   **communi' corruptela** Demea hails his approaching brother as the joint corrupter of his two sons. He has Micio where he wants him, caught barehanded in his misdeeds. Micio's reply evades his guilt and turns into an attack on the expected fury of Demea. Not fair.

795-99   Showing changes in his behavior, Demea quickly disposes of the two verbs in what Micio said in 794. Instead of ranting, as you expect of me, let's think this situation over. It was originally Micio's idea, that he would have complete independence in bringing Aeschinus up. It followed that Demea would not allow interference in his work with Ctesipho. Micio can only admit the truth in those words. If so, demands Demea, why is Ctesipho in your house now drinking?

800-805 Now, he refers to the girl, rightly accusing Micio of having bought her for Ctesipho. Another direct question follows, with its *numqui* to determine its answer: No. If Micio admits there should be fair dealings between the brothers, Demea replies: then why are you butting into my business? Micio does not back down, He denies the fairness of Demea's argument and falls back on an old proverb, which sounds fine, but is very questionable. "All things are possessed in common among friends." We can easily imagine exceptions. Plainly, Micio has overstepped the line and excused himself very lamely. Demea sneers: how clever! (805).

806-11 Instead of defending the adage, Micio launches into a lordly monetary argument. He claims he will speak *paucis* (*verbis*), but he controls the discussion for nearly thirty lines. So first (*principio*), the expenses of the boys in spite of Demea's teachings and remonstrances. Micio wants Demea to look at them from his personal angle (808). That is based on the different life styles and goals that he and Demea live by. Demea had married and had two sons whom he intended to bring up as well as possible, and he had no plan to exploit Micio, because he expected Micio eventually to marry, too (811). Money has not been the main problem of Demea with his sons. Micio has started on the (for him) easier argument.

812-19 **rationem antiquam optine** "Stick to your original plan." Overstating the situation, Micio then piles up four imperatives (813–14) of similar meaning, that emphasize saving more than Demea does and thus sound ironic and mildly critical.

814 **gloriam** Micio continues his irony: When you die, leave them a pile as an inheritance and gain the reputation you seek thereby. It doesn't sound much like "glory" when put that way. Micio is rigging the argument so that he gets the glory for helping the two boys in their extravagant wishes and behavior.

815 **mea** acc. pl. with *utantur*, instead of abl. *meis*.

praeter spem What the boys get from Micio will be like an unexpected bonus, and it will not deduct from Demea's capital.

817   **putato** fut. imperative: just think of it as profit on an invest-
ment. Micio then summarizes (817–19) by urging that, if Demea can reason in Micio's way, he will free himself of a great
deal of anxiety. Perhaps, but, as noted, Demea was not hypno-
tized by money as much as Micio seems to be.

820-25 Micio winds down on the monetary argument, which is not
the principal objection held by Demea, and that lets Demea
try to introduce his problem with his brother.

820   **mitto rem** "I leave aside the material theme." He starts to state
what his real concern is, namely, the habits and character of
his sons. But before he can develop his point in his own words,
Micio interrupts.

821-25 **istuc ibam** "I was getting there." But not really. Micio ignores
the objection Demea has against his interferences and proposes instead that each of the boys is a paragon, from whom
great expectations are valid. He starts with a grandiose generalization: suppose you have two men doing the same thing. A
little observation will lead to the conclusion that one of them
can do the act without danger, whereas the other cannot. Why
not? Because they are not doing a dissimilar act, but they are
dissimilar men. Fine, and how does Micio apply this?

826-31 **quae (signa)** Here something goes wrong with Micio's argument. Instead of going on with the theme of dissimilarity, he
claims that all signs point to the (similar) honorable character
of both Aeschinus and Ctesipho. Since they are quite different in behavior and do quite dissimilar things, it is not clear
where Micio found his dream of their similarity. Having said
so much, Micio returns to the monetary theme and holds it
against Demea: the boys are, as Micio attributes to Demea, a
little too careless about material things.

831-35 With a patronizing apostrophe (831), Micio launches into
pedantry about a unique fault of aging (which he is attributing
to his older brother Demea invalidly). Materialism is a special
vice of age, but surely not the only vice, as Micio claims.

835   **quod illos sat aetas acuet** As the boys grow older, age will sharpen their avarice. So Demea really does not need to worry about their carelessness with money now.

835-40   **ne . . . subvortat** this long subjunctive clause understands a verb of fearing (e.g., *timeo*). Demea is sardonic about what he calls the "good" reasoning and "generous" mind of Micio. Later, when he has reversed positions of power in the family, Demea mocks Micio for being too avaricious himself.

839   **exporge frontem** "smooth the scowl from your forehead"

scilicet ita tempus fert "I suppose the occasion demands it." Demea goes on reluctantly: "It must be done."

840-45   After making an effort to erase his scowl, Demea consoles himself by truculently declaring that he will take Ctesipho off to the country farm the first thing in the morning. Micio teases him, advising him to leave in the middle of the night (*de nocte*). But for this day Demea should force himself to be cheerful. Demea, however, has further plans: he is going to drag to the farm the girl dancer whom Ctesipho has acquired. That will fix her: an urban slut forced to do farm work! Micio again comments ironically: "You'll win the war."

844   **illi** refers to *psaltriae*

845   **facito** fut. imperative introducing subjunctive of indirect command. "Just be sure to keep her on the farm."

845-49   Demea gloats over his plans to ruin the romantic attractions of the girl. Reduced to the role of working maid, she will be smeared with soot, smoke, and flour. Then, at high noon, the hottest time, she will be forced out in the brutal sun to collect straw, so that her complexion will be cooked and she turn "black as coal."

850-54   Micio reacts with a show of approval. He has one more refinement: Ctesipho, even if he doesn't want to, will be compelled every night to sleep with his much-altered girlfriend. Even Demea realizes that he is being mocked, and he resents it.

852   **qui isto animo sies** subjunctive in relative clause of characteristic. "You're lucky to be taking all this so frivolously." Then, he goes on: "But I feel it." Micio won't let Demea go on in that mood, and he agrees to calm down. The final words of this scene are Micio's. The text has been much emended to produce the sense: "for this occasion, let us use this day." Micio seems to have won out over Demea, but he will soon be paying his penalty.

After his brother has gone into the house, Micio follows, well satisfied with his achievement; and the stage is empty while we assume that the celebrations are going well. Suddenly, Demea emerges by no means mollified, and in a long soliloquy he at last gets to state his case and to raise pertinent questions about Micio and his deserts. The meter is trochaic septenarius, a steady set of eight beats to reflect Demea's strong emotions.

855-61   This is the first time in the play where Demea has been calm and reflective. He points out soon that he is a changed man. But he begins with a thematic statement of how he has come to realize that nobody can really control events without facing some sudden reversals of understanding.

859   **vitam duram . . . iam decurso spatio omitto** He applies the generalization to himself. He had lived by choice a tough life that would give him the results he desired. Now, however, as he has almost reached the end of the race of life, he is abandoning that lifestyle. Why? He has discovered, he says, that nothing is better for a man than affability and mildness.

862-65   Demea proposes to prove this new discovery by comparing his life with that of his brother. Micio has lived his life at leisure, attending parties, mild and peaceful with everyone, never insulting anyone, laughing at or with everyone.

864   **laedere . . . adridere** historic infinitives. Micio lived for himself, behavior which we have come to suspect.

865   "He spent on himself": this seems to be an exaggeration of Micio's free-spending, because we have seen him bailing both Aeschinus and Ctesipho out of financial trouble. And he is paying for this party today, only indirectly for himself.

866-71 In contrast with Micio's success, Demea will now view his own life as a wretched failure.

866   **ego ille** With a series of six adjectives, Demea summarizes his life as others looked at him. This line comes from Menander's play, and Terence has ingeniously rewritten the Greek iambics as a trochaic septenarius. The traits he lists, while forming a striking contrast with the mildness of Micio, emphasize the antisocial effect of Demea's harshness on himself and the pleasures of life. He goes on to mention his marriage, which was misery for himself. He married partly to have sons, and two were born, but gloomy Demea now calls what he planned and desired only more anxiety (*alia cura*, 868). While he tried to do the best he could for the two sons, he essentially failed to acquire much and of course had to give Aeschinus up to adoption; he now realizes that he ruined his life. So what is his reward for all that effort at the end of his life? Simply put, hatred. Micio enjoys all the advantages of paternity without any of the toil that has exhausted Demea.

872-76 For all Demea's *labor*, he gets dislike and solitude, while Micio, at little expense and with a big show of *clementia*, has won affection from his, Demea's sons. It is bad enough to admit that Aeschinus loves Micio. What really hurts is the fact that Ctesipho loves him, too. Micio has stolen the love of his sons, in spite of Demea's hard work (*labore maxumo*, 875) and for a paltry sum (*paullo sumptu*, 876).

877-81 This is the final step in Demea's transformation. Now at last, when he realizes how easy and cheap it was for Micio to win over his two sons, he decides to make his life over and imitate his brother. It is a kind of competition or duel. He reduces the change in his behavior to speaking amiably (*blande dicere*) and acting amiably (*benigne facere*). That will earn him love.

879   **magni pendi** The adjective is genitive of value; the verb seems
to be a conjecture for a disputed text. Demea wants to be
weighed in the scales as of importance. If love can be won by
giving presents and money and by backing the sons in their
need, well that seems pretty easy, only a matter of money.

880   **non posteriores feram** an acting metaphor ("I shall not play a
secondary role."). This is now Demea's comedy, and he insists
on the lead.

881   **deerit** The only problem with Demea's transformation and
competition with Micio in spending is that sooner or later
they are going to run out of money, since nobody will be
working and saving and everybody is spending. But what the
Hell, declares Demea. I am the eldest and least affected by this
eventual shortage of funds. As eldest, he has the first rights to
the family funds.

There are many questions about how Terence ended this
play, whether and how much he altered the original Greek of
Menander. What he does is show Demea flaunting his easy-
going generosity at the expense of Micio, who grows more
and more irritated at the disposal of his property and even his
person: the lifelong bachelor is compelled by Demea and the
sons to marry Sostrata, the mother of Aeschinus' wife. Demea
tampers with the servants of Micio, liberating them and giving them Micio's money to start out in life again. The sons are
quickly taken in by the improvements in their grouchy father,
but the audience should not be, it appears. Demea does not
fully subscribe to a life of free expenses, nor does he want his
sons to idealize the easy-going way. But he has learned some
things about himself that he can use wisely.

Appendix

∾ *Comic Meters in Terence*

Most Plautine plays and just about all Terence's are written in either iambic or trochaic lines, which were felt to represent ordinary
speech. The two most common lines are the iambic senarius (Latin
version of Greek iambic trimeter) and the trochaic septenarius (Latin
version of the trochaic tetrameter catalectic, which Menander uses
sparingly). The Romans allowed considerably more freedom than
the Greeks had done, and we must be prepared for frequent elision
and substitution for iamb and trochee in every foot except the last.

Basic senarius (6 iambs)

    – ⏑̅| – ⏑̅| – ⏑̅| ⏑⏑̅|⏑ ⏑̅|⏑⏑̅

    vos istaec intro auferte: abite.—Sosia   (*Andria* 28)

Basic septenarius (7.5 trochees)

    ⏑̅ – | ⏑̅ ⏑| ⏑̆ ⏑ ⏑|⏑̆⏑– | ⏑̅   – |⏑̅–|⏑̅ ⏑| ⏑̅

    sed non credidi adeo ut etiam totam hanc odisset domum.

                                           (*Hecyra* 221)

The following may be substituted:

	For an iamb	For a trochee
Tribrach	⏑ ⏑̆ ⏑	⏑̆ ⏑ ⏑
Spondee	– ⏑̅	⏑̅ –
Anapest	⏑ ⏑ ⏑̅	⏑̆ ⏑ –
Dactyl	– ⏑̆ ⏑	⏑̅ ⏑ ⏑
Proceleusmatic	⏑ ⏑ ⏑̆ ⏑	⏑̆ ⏑ ⏑ ⏑
	NEVER A TROCHEE	NEVER AN IAMB

So here is a sequence of **iambic senarii** lines scanned from Terence's first play, *Andria*. It was unaccompanied by flute, and spoken; used in about fifty percent of Terence's lines for scenes of dialogue.

⏑ ‒́ | ‒   ‒́| ‒ ‒́ | ⏑ ‒́ | ‒ ‒́ | ⏑ ‒́
29   Ades dum: paucis te volo. Dictum puta:

‒   ‒́ | ‒ ‒́ | ‒   ‒́ | ‒   ‒́ | ⏑⏑ ‒́ | ⏑   ‒́
Nempe ut curentur recte haec? Immo aliud. Quid est

‒ ⏑⏑ | ⏑ ‒́ | ‒⏑⏑| ‒   ‒́ | ⏑ ‒́ | ⏑‒́
Quod tibi mea ars efficere hoc possit amplius?

⏑ ‒́| ‒ ⏑⏑ | ‒ ‒́ | ⏑   ‒ |‒   ‒́ | ⏑ ‒́
Nil istac opus est arte ad hanc rem quam paro,

⏑ ⏑‒́ | ‒ ‒́ | ⏑ ‒́ | ‒ ‒́|‒ ‒́|⏑ ‒́
33   Sed eis quae semper in te intellexi sitas.

Here, by contrast, is a sequence of **trochaic septenarii** lines scanned from his *Hecyra*. It was accompanied by flutists on one or two pipes and sung or intoned. It was especially used for recitative.

‒́ ⏑ ⏑ | ‒́ ⏑⏑ | ‒́ ⏑|‒́   ‒ |⏑⏑ ‒ | ‒́ ‒ | ‒́ ⏑|‒́
223   At vide quam inmerito aegritudo haec oritur mi abs te, Sostrata:

‒́   ⏑⏑|‒́   ⏑⏑|‒ | ‒́ ‒ | ‒́ ‒|‒́ ‒|‒́ ⏑|‒́
Rus habitatum abii concedens vobis et rei serviens.

‒́   ‒ | ‒́ ‒ |‒́⏑|‒́   ‒|‒́   ⏑|‒́ ‒|‒́ ⏑|‒́
Sumptus vostros otiumque ut nostra res posset pati,

‒́ ⏑|‒́ ‒ | ‒́ ‒ | ‒́ ⏑|‒́   ‒| ‒́‒|‒́ ⏑|‒́
Meo labori haud parcens praeter aequom atque aetatem meam.

‒́ ‒ | ‒́ ‒|‒́ ⏑|‒́ ‒| ‒́ ⏑ |‒́   ‒|‒́ ⏑|‒́
227   Non te pro his curasse rebus nequid aegre esset mihi!

Plautus also frequently used the iambic septenarius (7 iambs) as well as many different lyric meters. Terence abandons lyric, but he employs iambic septenarius and even more commonly iambic octonarius (8 iambs). Here are three lines from a soliloquy of the unhappy son in the *Heauton* that illustrate Terence's skill with the **iambic octonarius**:

213 Quam iniqui sunt patres in omnis adulescentis iudices!

Qui aequom esse censent nos a pueris ilico nasci senes

215 Neque illarum adfinis esse rerum quas fert adulescentia.

Vocabulary

ā, *see* **ab**

ab/abs, *prep.* + *abl.,* from, by

abdūcō, -ere, -xī, -ctum, to lead or take away

abeō, abīre, abīvī/abiī, abitum, to go away

abhinc, *adv.,* hence, from this time

abitiō, -ōnis, *f.,* a departure, a going way

abscēdō, -ere, -cessī, -cessum, to depart, go away

abstrahō, -ere, -traxī, -tractum, to drag away

absum, abesse, āfuī, —, to be away, be absent

ac, *conj.,* and

accēdō, -ere, -cessī, -cessum, to approach, come near

accersō, -ere, -īvī/-iī, -ītum, to fetch, summon

accipiō, -ere, -cēpī, -ceptum, to take, receive

accūsō (1), to accuse, blame

acuō, -ere, -uī, -ūtum, to sharpen, encourage

ad, *prep.* + *acc.,* to, towards

adbibō, -ere, -ī, —, to drink, drink in

adcurrō, -ere, -currī, -cursum, to run to, meet, clash

Adelphī, -ōrum, *proper noun,* the name of a play, Greek for *The Brothers*

adeō, *adv.,* so, so much, to such an extent

adeō, adīre, adiī, aditum, to go or come to, approach

adfectō (1), to strive after, aim for, affect, endow

adferō, adferre, attulī, allātum, to bring or carry to

adfīnis, -is, -e, *adj.,* neighboring, related (by marriage)

adfīnitās, -ātis, *f.,* a relationship by marriage

adgnoscō, -ere, -nōvī, -nitum, to recognize, acknowledge

adgredior, -ī, -ssus sum, to approach, go to

adhortor, -ārī, -ātus sum, to encourage, exhort

adhūc, *adv.,* up to this time, still

adimō, -ere, -ēmī, -emptum, to take away

adiungō, -ere, -iunxī, -iunctum, to join to, apply

adiūrō (1), to swear

adiūtō (1), to help

adligō (1), to tie or bind to

admittō, -ere, -mīsī, -missum, to allow, let in

adnuō, -ere, -nuī, -nūtum, to nod to, agree

adornō (1), to prepare, adorn

adparō (1), to prepare, get ready, provide

adportō (1), to carry or bring to

adprīmē, *adv.,* above all, exceedingly

adrīdeō, -ēre, -sī, -sum, to smile upon, be pleasing

adsequor, -ī, -cūtus sum, to follow after, reach

adsiduē, *adv.,* continually, constantly

adsimulō (1), to pretend

adspectō (1), to look at

adsum, adesse, adfuī, —, to be present, be at or near

adtentior, -ior, -ius, *compar. adj.,* more or quite attentive, careful

adulescens, -ntis, *adj.,* young; *m./f.,* a young man or woman

adulescentia, -ae, *f.,* youth

adulescentulus, -a, -um, *adj.,* very young; *m./f.,* a very young man or woman

adveniō, -īre, -vēnī, -ventum, to come to, arrive

adversus, *adv. and prep. + acc.,* opposed to, against

advorsārius, -a, -um, *adj.,* opposed; *m./f.,* an opponent, a rival

advorsor, -ārī, -ātus sum, to oppose, resist

advortō, -ere, -vortī, -vorsum, to turn toward, direct; *pass.,* to be turned away, opposed, unfavorable to

aedēs, -ium, *f. pl.,* a house

aedīlis, -is curūlis, -is, *m.,* curule aedile (a Roman magistrate)

aeger, -gra, -grum, *adj.,* sick

aegrē, *adv.,* with reluctance or difficulty

aegritūdō, -inis, *f.,* sickness, difficulty

aequālis, -is, *m.,* a peer

aequanimitās, -ātis, *f.,* impartiality

aequē, *adv.,* in a like manner

aequos, -a, -om, *adj.,* equal, fair

aetās, -ātis, *f.,* age, time, a lifetime

agō, agere, ēgī, actum, to do, drive, give, have dealings, spend (time)

agrestis, -is, -e, *adj.,* rustic, boorish

āh, *interj.,* an expression of various feelings (distress, joy, etc.)

āiō, *defective verb,* to say, assert

Albīnus, -ī, *m.,* a Roman name

aliēnus, -a, -um, *adj.,* belonging or relating to another, not one's own

aliquantus, -a, -um, *adj.,* some amount

aliquī, -qua, -quod, *adj.,* some

aliquis, -qua, -quid, *pron.,* someone, something, anyone, anything

aliquot, *indecl. adj.,* some, several

alius, -a, -ud, *adj.,* another, other, different

alō, -ere, -uī, -tum/-itum, to nourish, rear

alter, -era, -erum, *adj.,* one of two, the other

Ambivius, -ī, *m.,* a Roman name

ambō, -ae, -ō, *adj.,* both

ambulō (1), to walk, go

amīcus, -a, -um, *adj.,* friendly; *m./f.,* a friend (male or female)

āmittō, -ere, -mīsī, -missum, to send away, lose

amō (1), to love

amor, -ōris, *m.,* love

amplius, *compar. adv.,* more, in addition

an, *particle,* or, whether

ancilla, -ae, *f.,* a female slave

ancillula, -ae, *f.,* a little slave girl

Andrius, -a, -um, *adj.,* from Andrus

Andrus, -ī, *f.,* a Greek island

angiportum, -ī, *n.,* a narrow street

animus, -ī, *m.,* the mind, heart

annus, -ī, *m.,* a year

anteā, *adv.,* before, formerly

Antiphō, -ōnis, *m.,* a Greek name

antīquos, -a, -om, *adj.,* earlier, ancient

ānulus, -ī, *m.,* a ring

anus, -ūs, *f.,* an old woman

aperiō, -īre, -uī, -tum, to uncover, reveal, open

apertē, *adv.,* openly

apud, *prep.* + *acc.,* at, near, by, with, among

arbitror, -ārī, -ātus sum, to perceive, judge, think

argentārius, -a, -um, *adj.,* relating to silver, financial

argentum, -ī, *n.,* silver, money

argūmentum, -ī, *n.,* a proof, the subject matter, contents

arripiō, -ere, -ripuī, -reptum, to seize, lay hold of, snatch

ars, -tis, *f.,* skill

Asia, -ae, *f.,* Asia Minor

asinus, -ī, *m.,* an ass, idiot

aspiciō, -ere, -spexī, -spectum, to look at

asportō (1), to carry off, take away

astūtē, *adv.,* cleverly

astūtus, -a, -um, *adj.,* clever, crafty

at, *conj.,* but

āter, ātra, ātrum, *adj.,* black, dark

Athēnae, -ārum, *f.,* Athens

Atīlius, -ī, *m.,* a Roman name

atque, *conj.,* and

attamen, *conj.,* but nevertheless

attat, *interj.,* oh! (an expression of surprise or fear)

attendō, -ere, -dī, -tum, to stretch to, be attentive

attineō, -ēre, -tinuī, -tentum, to hold, pertain to

audācia, -ae, *f.,* boldness, daring, recklessness

audiō, -īre, -īvī/-iī, -ītum, to hear, listen to

auferō, auferre, abstulī, ablātum, to carry away or off, remove, steal

augeō, -ēre, -xī, -ctum, to increase

aureus, -a, -um, *adj.,* golden

aurum, -ī, *n.,* gold

auscultō (1), to listen, overhear

aut, *conj.,* or

autem, *particle,* however, moreover

bellum, -ī, *n.,* war

bene, *adv.,* well

beneficium, -ī, *n.,* a favor, service

benignē, *adv.,* kindly, generously

benignitās, -ātis, *f.,* kindness, generosity

beō (1), to be happy, lucky

blandē, *adv.,* flatteringly

bonus, -a, -um, *adj.,* good

brevis, -is, -e, *adj.,* brief, short

caedō, -ere, cecīdī, caesum, to cut, lash, beat

caelum, -ī, *n.,* the sky

canis, -is, *m./f.,* a dog

capiō, -ere, cēpī, captum, to take, seize, receive

carbō, -ōnis, *m.,* charcoal

causa, -ae, *f.,* a cause, reason, case

caveō, -ēre, cāvī, cautum, to be on guard, take care, provide

cedo, *imperative,* give!

cēlō (1), to hide, keep secret

cēna, -ae, *f.,* dinner

cēnō (1), to have dinner, eat

censeō, -ēre, -uī, -um, to think, judge

cernō, -ere, crēvī, crētum, to distinguish, decide

certē, *adv.,* certainly

certō, *adv.,* certainly

certus, -a, -um, *adj.,* decided, fixed, sure

cessō (1), to leave off, delay, do nothing

cēterus, -a, -um, *adj.,* the other, the rest

cēterum, *adv.,* but

Chaerea, -ae, *m.,* a Greek name

Chremēs, -ētis, *m.,* a Greek name

Chrysis, -idis, *f.,* a Greek name

circum, *prep. + acc.,* around

circumspectō, -āre, —, —, to look around at

citior, -or, -us, *compar. adj.,* more quickly, rather quickly

clam, *adv.,* secretly; *prep. + abl.,* unknown to

clāmō (1), to shout, call to, proclaim

clanculum, *adv.,* secretly; *prep. + abl.,* unknown to

Claudius, -ī, *m.,* a Roman name

clēmens, -ntis, *adj.,* kind, merciful

clēmentia, -ae, *f.,* kindness, mercy

Clīnia, -ae, *m.,* a Greek name

Clitiphō, -ōnis, *m.,* a Greek name

coeō, coīre, coiī, coitum, to go or come together, assemble

coepī, coepisse, —, coeptum, to begin

cōgitō (1), to think over, consider, plan

cognātus, -a, -um, *adj.,* related by blood

cognōscō, -ere, -nōvī, -nitum, to get to know, learn

cōgō, -ere, coēgī, coactum, to bring together, compel, force

comedō, -esse/-edere, -ēdī, -ēs(s)um, to eat up, consume

Commorientēs, -um, *proper noun,* the name of a play, *Those Who Die Together*

commeminī, -isse, —, —, to remember fully

commemorātiō, -ōnis, *f.,* a reminding, mention

commendō (1), to commit to the care of someone, recommend

commigrō (1), to migrate, move

committō, -ere, -mīsī, -missum, to entrust, combine

commodus, -a, -um, *adj.,* in full measure, proper; *n.,* advantage

commoveō, -ēre, -ōvī, -ōtum, to move violently, alarm, disturb

commūnis, -is, -e, *adj.,* shared, common, universal

cōmoedia, -ae, *f.,* a comedy

comperiō, -īre, -ī, -tum, to find out, discover

complector, -ī, -xus sum, to embrace, hold tight

concēdō, -ere, -cessī, -cessum, to go away, withdraw, give up, grant

conclāve, -is, *n.,* a room

concurrō, -ere, -currī, -cursum, to run together, meet, clash

concutiō, -ere, -cussī, -cussum, to shake, agitate

condiciō, -ōnis, *f.,* an arrangement, agreement, condition

condōnō (1), to give away, present

confīdō, -ere, -fīsus sum, to have complete trust, believe firmly

conflictō (1), to strike together, collide

cōniciō, -ere, -iēcī, -iectum, to throw together, guess

coniectō (1), to throw together, guess

coniectūra, -ae, *f.,* a guess, inference

coniunx, -ugis, *m./f.,* a spouse

coniūrātiō, -ōnis, *f.,* a union bonded by oath, conspiracy

conlacrumō (1), to weep together, weep very much

conligō, -ere, -lēgī, -lectum, to bind together, connect, hinder

conlocō (1), to place, arrange, settle

cōnor, -ārī, -ātus sum, to try, attempt

consequor, -ī, -cūtus sum, to follow, pursue, reach, attain

conservō (1), to keep, preserve, save

consilium, -ī, *n.,* a deliberation, plan

consimilis, -is, -e, *adj.,* exactly similar

constituō, -ere, -uī, -ūtum, to set up, establish, decide

consuescō, -ere, -suēvī, -suētum, to accustom, get used to

consuētūdō, -inis, *f.,* custom, usage, habit

consul, -is, *m.,* Rome's highest magistrate

contāminō (1), to pollute, blend

contemnō, -ere, -tempsī, -temptum, to despise, be contemptuous of

conterō, -ere, -trīvī, -trītum, to wear away, grind, trample

continentia, -ae, *f.,* self-control, moderation

continuō, *adv.,* immediately, at once

contrā, *adv.,* opposite, against, otherwise

contumēlia, -ae, *f.,* abuse, an insult

conveniō, -īre, -vēnī, -ventum, to come together, meet, fit, agree

convīvium, -ī, *n.,* a feast, dinner-party

convīvor, -ārī, -ātus sum, to feast, party

convortō, -ere, -tī, -sum, to turn around or back

coquō, -ere, coxī, coctum, to cook

cōram, *adv.,* openly, publicly, face-to-face

Cornēlius, -ī, *m.,* a Roman name

corrigō, -ere, -rexī, -rectum, to straighten, order, set right

corrumpō, -ere, -rūpī, -ruptum, to completely break, destroy, corrupt

corruptēla, -ae, *f.,* corruption, corrupter

crās, *adv.,* tomorrow

crēbrō, *adv.,* repeatedly, often

credō, -ere, -didī, -ditum, to trust, entrust, believe

cubō, -āre, -uī, -itum, to lie down, recline

culpa, -ae, *f.,* fault, blame

cum, *prep. + abl.,* with

cupiditās, -ātis, *f.,* desire, longing

cupiō, -ere, -īvī/-iī, -itum, to desire, long for

cūra, -ae, *f.,* care, concern

cūriōsus, -a, -um, *adj.,* careful, inquisitive

cūrō (1), to care for, pay attention to

Danaē, -ēs, *f.,* a Greek name

dē, *prep. + abl.,* down, from, about

dea, -ae, *f.,* a goddess

dēbeō, -ēre, -uī, -itum, to owe, ought to

dēcēdō, -ere, -cessī, -cessum, to go away, yield, withdraw

dēcernō, -ere, -crēvī, -crētum, to decide, determine, settle

decet, -ēre, -uit, —, *impers.*, it is proper, fitting

dēcīdō, -ere, -dī, -sum, to cut down, cut off, cut short

dēcipiō, -ere, -cēpī, -ceptum, to catch, cheat, deceive

dēclīnō (1), to turn away, swerve

dēcurrō, -ere, -cursī/-cucursī, -cursum, to run down, run towards, run through

dēdecorō (1), to dishonor, bring shame onto

dēdō, -ere, -didī, -ditum, to give up, surrender

dēdūcō, -ere, -xī, -ctum, to lead or bring down, to lead or bring away

dehinc, *adv.*, from here, from this time

dehortor, -ārī, -ātus sum, to discourage, dissuade

dein/deinde, *adv.*, then, next

dēlapidō (1), to pave over, take stones from

Dēmea, -ae, *m.*, a Greek name

Demiphō, -ōnis, *m.*, a Greek name

dēmō, -ere, -mpsī, -mptum, to take away

dēmum, *adv.*, at last, finally

dēnarrō (1), to narrate, tell, relate

dērīdeō, -ēre, -sī, -sum, to laugh at, mock

dēserō, -ere, -uī, -tum, to desert, abandon, leave, neglect

dēsinō, -ere, -sīvī/-siī, -situm, to leave off, cease, stop

despondeō, -ēre, -dī, -sum, to pledge, promise (in marriage)

dēsum, -esse, -fuī, —, to fall short, fail

dētrīmentum, -ī, *n.*, loss, damage, injury

deus, deī, *m.*, a god

dēvinciō, -īre, -xī, -ctum, to bind, tie tightly, attach

dexter, -tra, -trum, *adj.*, right, the right hand, on the right hand side

dīcō, -ere, -xī, -ctum, to say, speak, tell

dictum, -ī, *n.*, a word, saying, speech

diēs, diēī, *m.*, a day

dignus, -a, -um, *adj.*, worthy, deserving

dīiūdicō (1), to judge between parties, decide

dīligenter, *adv.*, carefully, attentively

dīligentia, -ae, *f.*, care, attentiveness

dīligō, -ere, -lexī, -lectum, to choose, prize, love, value

Dīphilus, -ī, *m.*, a Greek name

Discus, -ī, *m.*, a Greek name

discrībō, -ere, -psī, -ptum, to divide up (in writing), distribute, allot

dissimilis, -is, -e, *adj.*, unlike, different

dissimulō (1), to hide, disguise, keep secret, pretend

dītiae, -ārum, *f. pl., contraction of* **dīvitiae, -arum,** riches, wealth

dō, dare, dedī, datum, to give, offer

doctus, -a, -um, *adj.,* instructed, well-informed, experienced, clever

dominus, -ī, *m.,* master, head of the household

domus, -ūs/-ī, *f.,* house, household

dōnum, -ī, *n.,* a gift, present

Dōris, -idis, *m.,* a Greek name

dōs, dōtis, *f.,* a dowry

dōtātus, -a, -um, *adj.,* provided with a dowry

Dromō, -ōnis, *m.,* a Greek name

dūcō, -ere, -xī, -ctum, to lead, reckon

dūdum, *adv.,* a while, some time ago

dulcis, -is, -e, *adj.,* sweet, pleasant

dum, *adv.,* yet, now; *conj.,* while (+ *indicative*), provided that (+ *subjunctive*)

duo, -ae, -o, *adj.,* two

dūrus, -a, -um, *adj.,* hard, tough

ē, *see* **ex**

ēbibō, -ere, -ī, -itum, to drink up

eccōs, *interj.,* look!, here they are!

eccum, *interj.,* look!, here he is!

ecferō, ecferre, extulī, ēlātum, to carry or bring out, carry off, lift up

ecquis, ecquid, *interr. pron.,* does anyone?, anything?

edepol, *interj.,* by Pollux!

ēdīcō, -ere, -xī, -ctum, to announce, declare

ēducō (1), to bring up, rear, educate

ēdūcō, -ere, -xī, -ctum, to lead out, raise up, rear, spend time

efficiō, -ere, -fēcī, -fectum, to do, produce, bring about

ego, meī, *pers. pron.,* I, me

ēgredior, -ī, -essus sum, to go out, go up

ēgregiē, *adv.,* excellently, outstandingly

ēgregius, -a, -um, *adj.,* excellent, outstanding

eho, *interj.,* hey!, you!

ei, *interj.,* oh!, oh no! (an expression of distress)

ēlegans, -ntis, *adj.,* tasteful, fine, fussy

ēloquor, -ī, -cūtus sum, to speak out, express

ēlūdō, -ere, -sī, -sum, to finish playing, evade, ward off

em, *interj.,* hey!, look!

ēmergō, -ere, -mersī, -mersum, to rise up, come forth, emerge

emō, -ere, ēmī, emptum, to buy

ēmorior, -ī, -tuos sum, to die off

ēnicō, -āre, -āvī/-uī, -tum, to kill off, wear out

enim, *particle,* indeed, certainly, for instance

enimvērō, *particle,* to be sure, certainly

eō, *adv.,* to that point, for that reason

eō, īre, īvī/iī, itum, to go, come

ephēbus, -ī, *m.,* Greek for a young man

equidem, *particle,* indeed, for my part, certainly

equus, -ī, *m.,* a horse

ergā, *prep. + acc.,* towards

ergō, *particle,* consequently, therefore, then

ēripiō, -ere, -ripuī, -reptum, to snatch, snatch away, tear out, rescue

ērumpō, -ere, -rūpī, -ruptum, to break open, break out

et, *conj.,* and; *adv.,* even, also

etiam, *particle,* still, also, yes

etiamdum, *particle,* yet, already

etiamnunc, *particle,* yet, still, till now

etsī, *conj.,* even if, although

Eunūchus, -ī, *m.,* the name of a play, Greek for *The Castrated Man* or *The Eunuch*

ēvādō, -ere, -sī, -sum, to go out, climb up, escape

ēveniō, -īre, -vēnī, -ventum, to come out, turn out, result

ēvocō (1), to call out, summon

ex, *prep. + abl.,* from, out of

exanimātus, -a, -um, *adj.,* breathless, dead

exaugeō, -ēre, —, —, to increase greatly

excēdō, -ere, -cessī, -cessum, to go out, go away, go beyond

exclūdō, -ere, -sī, -sum, to shut out, exclude, knock out, prevent

excoquō, -ere, -coxī, -coctum, to boil down, boil away, cook up

excruciō (1), to torture, torment greatly

exemplum, -ī, *n.,* an example, model, manner

exeō, exīre, exīvī/exiī, exitum, to go out, go away

exigō, -ere, -ēgī, -actum, to drive out, complete, spend

exiguē, *adv.,* sparingly, scarcely

existumō (1), to judge, consider, regard

exorior, -īrī, -tus sum, to rise up, spring up, arise, appear

experior, -īri, -tus sum, to try out, test, find out, discover

explōrō (1), to search out, investigate, examine, explore

exporgō, exporrigere, -rexī, -rectum, *contraction of* **exporrigō,** to stretch out, expand, smooth out

exprimō, -ere, -pressī, -pressum, to press out, express, translate

exprobrātiō, -ōnis, *f.,* reproach

expurgō (1), to cleanse, purify, cure, justify

exspectō (1), to look out for, wait for

exstillō, -āre, -āvī, —, to drip, trickle

exsulō (1), to be banished, live in exile

extrā, *adv.*, outside, beyond
extrūdō, **-ere**, **-sī**, **-sum**, to push out

fābula, **-ae**, *f.*, talk, a story, a play
faciēs, **-iēī**, *f.*, form, face, appearance.
facile, *adv.*, easily, without difficulty
facilis, **-is**, **-e**, *adj.*, easy, good-natured
facilitās, **-ātis**, *f.*, ease, friendliness
facillumē, *adv.*, most easily
facinus, **-oris**, *n.*, a deed, action, crime
faciō, **-ere**, **fēcī**, **factum**, to do, make
factum, **-ī**, *n.*, a deed, action
falsus, **-a**, **-um**, *adj.*, wrong, mistaken, false, deceitful
fāma, **-ae**, *f.*, rumor, (bad) reputation, public opinion
familia, **-ae**, *f.*, a household
familiāritās, **-ātis**, *f.*, familiarity, intimacy, friendship
familiāriter, *adv.*, familiarly, intimately, in a friendly way
Fannius, **-ī**, *m.*, a Roman name
fateor, **-ērī**, **fassus sum**, to confess, admit
fatuus, **-a**, **-om**, *adj.*, foolish, stupid, silly
favilla, **-ae**, *f.*, ashes
fēmina, **-ae**, *f.*, a woman, female
fermē, *adv.*, almost, nearly, hardly

ferō, **ferre**, **tulī**, **lātum**, to carry, bring, endure
festus, **-a**, **-um**, *adj.*, festive
fidēs, **-ēī**, *f.*, trust, confidence, reliance, protection
fidicina, **-ae**, *f.*, a female lute or harp player
fīlia, **-ae**, *f.*, a daughter
fīlius, **-ī**, *m.*, a son
fīō, **fierī**, —, —, to be, become, happen
flābellulum, **-ī**, *n.*, a little fan
flābellum, **-ī**, *n.*, a fan
Flaccus, **-ī**, *m.*, a Roman name
flamma, **-ae**, *f.*, a flame, blaze, fire
fleō, **-ēre**, **-ēvī**, **-ētum**, to weep, lament, wail
forās, *adv.*, out, outdoors
forīs, *adv.*, out, outdoors
foris, **-is**, *f.*, a door, entrance
forma, **-ae**, *f.*, form, appearance, beauty
fors, **-tis**, *f.*, chance, luck
fortasse, *adv.*, perhaps
forte, *adv.*, by chance
fortūna, **-ae**, *f.*, chance, fate, fortune
fortūnātus, **-a**, **-um**, *adj.*, lucky, fortunate
forum, **-ī**, *n.*, an open square, market-place
frāter, **-tris**, *m.*, a brother
fremō, **-ere**, **-uī**, **-itum**, to roar, murmur
frequens, **-ntis**, *adj.*, crowded, full, repeated, frequent
frētus, **-a**, **-um**, *adj.*, relying on, confiding in

frons, -ntis, *f.,* the forehead, front

fructus, -ūs/-ī, *m.,* enjoyment, profit, fruit

frūgī, *indecl. adj.,* useful, good, moderate

fūcus, -ī, *m.,* a dye, disguise, trick

fugitīvos, -a, -om, *adj.,* fugitive; *m./f.,* a runaway slave

fugitō, -āre, -āvī, —, to flee, avoid, shun

fūmus, -ī, *m.,* smoke, steam

fūnus, -eris, *n.,* a funeral, burial, corpse

furtum, -ī, *n.,* theft, robbery

Gaius, -ī, *m.,* a Roman name

gaudeō, -ēre, gāvīsus, to rejoice, be glad

gaudium, -ī, *n.,* joy, delight

genus, -eris, *n.,* a descent, race, family

gestiō, -īre, -īvī/-iī, —, to be excited, desire eagerly

gestus, -ūs, *m.,* posture, gestures, bearing

gladiātōrius, -a, -um, *adj.,* relating to gladiators

glōria, -ae, *f.,* fame, glory, ambition

Glycerium, -ī, *f.,* a Greek name

gnāta, -ae, *f.,* a daughter

gnātus, -ī, *m.,* a son

Graecus, -a, -um, *adj.,* Greek

grātia, -ae, *f.,* thanks, pleasantness, a favor

grātus, -a, -um, *adj.,* pleasing, grateful

graviter, *adv.,* heavily, harshly, seriously

gremium, -ī, *n.,* lap, bosom, womb

grex, gregis, *m.,* a herd, flock, troop

habeō, -ēre, -uī, -itum, to have, hold, consider

habitō (1), to inhabit, live

haereō, -ēre, -sī, -sum, to stick, cling, be stuck

haud, *particle,* not at all, by no means

haudquāquam, *adv.,* not at all, by no means

heia, *interj.,* oh, hey, well (an expression of various feelings: surprise, concession, etc.)

hem, *interj.,* well!, just look! (an expression of surprise or distress)

hercle, *interj.,* by Hercules!

heri, *adv.,* yesterday

heu, *interj.,* oh! (an expression of sorrow or regret)

heus, *interj.,* hey!

hīc, *adv.,* here

hic, haec, hoc, *adj.,* this

hilarus, -a, -um, *adj.,* cheerful

hinc, *adv.,* from here, hence, from this time

hodiē, *adv.,* today

homō, -inis, *m.,* a human, person, man

homunciō, -ōnis, *m.,* a little man, poor little man

honestē, *adv.,* respectably, honorably, properly

honestus, -a, -um, *adj.,* respectable, honorable, proper

honor, -ōris, *m.,* respect, honor, dignity

hūc, *adv.,* to here

hūmānus, -a, -um, *adj.,* human, humane, kind, refined

iam, *adv.,* now, already

iamdūdum, *adv.,* a while ago, long ago

iamprīdem, *adv.,* long ago

ibi, *adv.,* there

īdem, eadem, idem, *adj.,* the same one

ideō, *adv.,* for that reason, therefore

igitur, *conj.,* then, so then, therefore

ignārus, -a, -um, *adj.,* not knowing, unacquainted with

ignis, -is, *m.,* fire

ignōrō (1), to be ignorant of, not know

ignoscō, -ere, -nōvī, -nōtum, to overlook, forgive

īlicet, *adv.,* immediately, it's all over

īlicō, *adv.,* immediately, on the spot

ille, -a, -ud, *adj.,* that

illūc, *adv.,* to there

imber, -bris, *m.,* rain, a storm

immemor, -oris, *adj.,* unmindful, forgetful

immō, *particle,* rather, on the contrary

imperium, -ī, *n.,* a command, authority

imperō (1), to order, command

in, *prep.* + *acc.,* into, onto; + *abl.,* in, on

incensus, -a, -um, *adj.,* kindled, on fire

incertus, -a, -um, *adj.,* uncertain, doubtful

incipiō, -ere, -cēpī, -ceptum, to begin

incolumis, -is, -e, *adj.,* safe, uninjured

incūsō (1), to accuse, blame, find fault with

inde, *adv.,* from there, thence, then

indicium, -ī, *n.,* information, evidence

indicō (1), to make known, show, betray

indictus, -a, -um, *adj.,* declared, announced; unsaid, not said

indōtātus, -a, -um, *adj.,* not provided with a dowry

indūcō, -ere, -xī, -ctum, to lead over, bring in, introduce

industria, -ae, *f.,* diligent activity

ineō, inīre, inīvī/iniī, initum, to go or come in, enter

ineptus, -a, -um, *adj.,* unsuitable, tasteless, foolish

ingenium, -ī, *n.,* character, natural disposition, talent

ingerō, -ere, -gessī, -gestum, to put or throw upon

ingrātiīs, *f. abl. pl.,* unwillingly

inicio, -ere, -iēcī, -iectum, to throw in or onto

inimīcitia, -ae, *f.,* unfriendliness, hostility

inimīcus, -a, -um, *adj.,* unfriendly, hostile; *m./f.,* an enemy

inīquē, *adv.,* unequally, unfairly

inīquior, -ior, -ius, *compar. adj.,* more or quite unequal, unfair

inīquus, -a, -om, *adj.,* unequal, unfair

iniūria, -ae, *f.,* an injury, injustice, wrong

inlūdō, -ere, -sī, -sum, to play with, laugh at, mock

inmeritō, *adv.,* undeservedly

inopia, -ae, *f.,* poverty, a lack

inpedio, -īre, -īvī/-ii, -ītum, to entangle, ensnare, hinder

inpellō, -ere, -pulī, -pulsum, to drive against, drive on, strike upon

inpendio, *adv.,* greatly, very much

inpluvium, -ī, *n.,* an opening in the roof of the atrium

inpōnō, -ere, -posuī, -positum, to put or place on

inportūnus, -a, -um, *adj.,* unaccommodating, oppressive, troublesome

inprōvīsus, -a, -um, *adj.,* unforeseen, unexpected

inprudentius, *compar. adv.,* more or quite unwisely, unwittingly

inpudens, -ntis, *adj.,* shameless

inpudentia, -ae, *f.,* shamelessness

inpulsus, -ūs, *m.,* pressure, impulse, incitement

inpūne, *adv.,* with impunity, without punishment

inpūrātus, -a, -um, *adj.,* vile, filthy

inpūrus, -a, -um, *adj.,* dirty, vile, filthy

inquam, *defective verb,* to say

inrīdeō, -ēre, -sī, -sum, to laugh at, mock

insāniō, -īre, -īvī/-iī, -ītum, to be insane, rage, rave

insimulō (1), to charge, accuse

inspērātus, -a, -um, *adj.,* unhoped-for, unexpected

instīgō (1), to goad, incite

instituō, -ere, -uī, -ūtum, to put in place, set up

insum, inesse, infuī, —, to be inside, be within

integer, -gra, -grum, *adj.,* whole, complete, pure

intellegō, -ere, -exī, -ectum, to understand, perceive

inter, *prep. + acc.,* between, among

intereā, *adv.,* in the meantime, meanwhile

interficiō, -ere, -fēcī, -fectum, to do away with, put an end to, destroy, kill

interim, *adv.,* in the meantime, meanwhile, for the time being

interior, -or, -us, *adj.,* inner, interior

interveniō, -īre, -vēnī, -ventum, to come between, intervene, interrupt

intrō, *adv.*, inwards, within

intueor, -ērī, -itus sum, to look at attentively, contemplate

intus, *adv.*, inside, within

inveniō, -īre, -vēnī, -ventum, to come upon, find

invideō, -ēre, -vīsī, -vīsum, to envy, begrudge

invidia, -ae, *f.*, envy, unpopularity

invītō (1), to invite, summon

invītus, -a, -um, *adj.*, unwilling

ipse, -a, -um, *adj.*, himself, herself, itself, the very

ipsus, *see* ipse

īra, -ae, *f.*, anger

īrācundia, -ae, *f.*, anger, an angry disposition

īrātus, -a, -um, *adj.*, angry

irrītō (1), to stir up, excite, provoke, annoy

irritus, -a, -um, *adj.*, invalid, vain, useless

is, ea, id, *adj.*, this, that; *m./f./n.*, he, she, it

iste, -a, -ud, *adj.*, that, that of yours

istūc, *adv.*, to there, to that

ita, *adv.*, so, thus, in this way, certainly

itaque, *adv.*, and so, therefore

item, *adv.*, also, likewise

itidem, *adv.*, in the same way, likewise

iubeō, -ēre, iussī, iussum, to order, command

iūdex, -icis, *m.*, a judge

Iuppiter, Iovis, *m.*, Jupiter

iūs, iūris, *n.*, a right, law, court

iustus, -a, -um, *adj.*, just, lawful, fair

labor, -ōris, *m.*, work, labor, effort

Lachēs, -ētis, *m.*, a Greek name

lacruma, -ae, *f.*, a tear

laedō, -ere, laesī, laesum, to strike, knock, hurt, damage

laetitia, -ae, *f.*, joy, delight

laetor, -ārī, -ātus sum, to rejoice, be delighted

laetus, -a, -um, *adj.*, joyful, delighted

lāmentor, -ārī, -ātus sum, to weep, wail, lament

lāna, -ae, *f.*, wool

lapis, -idis, *m.*, a stone

lassus, -a, -um, *adj.*, worn out, tired, exhausted

laudō (1), to praise

laus, -dis, *f.*, praise, fame, glory

lautus, -a, -um, *adj.*, washed, splendid, fine, sumptuous

lavō, -āre/-ere, lāvī, lavātum/lautum, to wash, bathe

lectus, -ī, *m.*, a couch, bed

Lemnus, -ī, *f.*, a Greek island

lēnis, -is, -e, *adj.*, smooth, soft, gentle, mild

lēnō, -ōnis, *m.*, a pimp

lex, lēgis, *f.*, a law

līberālis, -is, -e, *adj.*, gentlemanlike, generous

līberāliter, *adv.*, gentlemanly, freely, generously

līberī, -um/-ōrum, *m. pl.,*
children

lībertus, -ī, *m.,* a freedman

licet, -ēre, -uit/-itum est,
impers., it is allowed,
permitted; + *subjunctive,*
although

līmis, -is, -e, *adj.,* looking
sideways, sidelong

līs, lītis, *f.,* a quarrel, lawsuit

locus, -ī, *m.,* a place

longius, *compar. adv.,* more or
quite long

longulē, *adv.,* somewhat far, at a
little distance

loquor, -ī, -cūtus sum, to speak,
say

lubens, -ntis, *adj.,* willingly,
freely, happily

lubet, -ēre, -itum est, *impers.,* it
is pleasing

lubīdō, -inis, *f.,* violent desire, lust

Lūcius, -ī, *m.,* a Roman name

lucrum, -ī, *n.,* gain, profit,
advantage

luctus, -ūs, *m.,* morning,
lamentation

lūdificor, -ārī, -ātus sum, to
laugh at, mock, cheat

lūdō, -ere, -sī, -sum, to play, do
for amusement

lūdus, -ī, *m.,* a game, pastime

lux, lūcis, *f., but m. here,* light,
daylight

mage, *see* **magis**

magis, *adv.,* more, rather

magister, -trī, *m.,* a master,
director, teacher (male)

magistra, -ae, *f.,* a master,
director, teacher (female)

magnificentia, -ae, *f.,* grandeur,
splendor, pomposity

magnificus, -a, -um, *adj.,*
grand, splendid, pompous

magnus, -a, -um, *adj.,* great

maledictum, -ī, *n.,* cursing, an
insult, mockery

malevolus, -a, -um, *adj.,*
spiteful, ill-disposed

malitia, -ae, *f.,* wickedness

malus, -a, -um, *adj.,* bad,
wicked

māne, *adv.,* in the morning

maneō, -ēre, -sī, -sum, to
remain, wait, stay

mansuēs, -ētis, *adj.,* tame,
gentle, mild

Marcus, -ī, *m.,* a Roman name

māter, -tris, *f.,* a mother

maxumē, *superl. adv.,* most
greatly, most of all,
especially, very.

maxumus, -a, -um, *superl. adj.,*
greatest

mediocriter, *adv.,* moderately,
not extraordinarily

medius, -a, -um, *adj.,* middle,
midst, middle portion

Megalensis, -is, -e, *adj.,* relating
or belonging to the Magna
Mater

melior, -or, -us, *compar. adj.,*
better

melius, *adv.,* better

memoria, -ae, *f.,* memory

Menander, -drū, *m.,* a Greek
name

Menedēmus, -ī, *m.*, a Greek name

mercātus, -ūs, *m.*, trade, business, a market

mercor, -ārī, -ātus sum, to carry on trade or traffic, to buy

meretrīcius, -a, -um, *adj.*, related or belonging to prostitutes

meretrix, -īcis, *f.*, a prostitute or courtesan

merīdiēs, -ēī, *m.*, midday, noon

meritō, *adv.*, deservedly

Merula, -ae, *m.*, a Roman name

-met, *enclitic particle that adds emphasis*

metuō, -ere, -uī, -ūtum, to fear, be afraid

metus, -ūs, *m.*, fear, apprehension

meus, -a, -um, *adj.*, my

Miciō, -ōnis, *m.*, a Greek name

mina, -ae, *f.*, a mina, a Greek form of currency worth 100 drachmas

minimē, *superl. adv.*, least, not at all

minus, *compar. adv.*, less

mīror, -ārī, -ātus sum, to wonder, be astonished, admire

mīrus, -a, -um, *adj.*, wonderful, astonishing

miser, -era, -erum, *adj.*, wretched, unhappy

miserē, *adv.*, wretchedly, unhappily, exceedingly

miseria, -ae, *f.*, wretchedness, unhappiness

misericordia, -ae, *f.*, pity, compassion, mercy

miserior, -ior, -ius, *compar. adj.*, more or quite wretched, unhappy

mittō, -ere, mīsī, missum, to send, let go, release

moderor, -ārī, -ātus sum, to set bounds, moderate, restrain

modestē, *adv.*, modestly, with restraint

modestus, -a, -um, *adj.*, modest, moderate, unassuming

modo, *adv.*, only, just

modus, -ī, *m.*, a measure, boundary, manner

molestia, -ae, *f.*, annoyance, troublesomeness

molestus, -a, -um, *adj.*, annoying, troublesome

mōlior, -īrī, -ītus sum, to labor, exert oneself

molō, -ere, -uī, -itum, to grind in a mill

moneō, -ēre, -uī, -itum, to warn, advise, remind

monstrum, -ī, *n.*, a wonder, portent, monster

morbus, -ī, *m.*, a disease, sickness

mordeō, -ēre, momordī, morsum, to bite

morior, -ī, -tuus sum, to die

moror, -ārī, -ātus sum, to delay, linger

mors, -tis, *f.*, death

mōs, mōris, *m.*, custom; *pl.*, character

mulier, -eris, *f.,* a woman
multimodīs, *adv.,* in many ways, variously
multus, -a, -um, *adj.,* much, many
mūtō (1), to move, change

-n, *see* **-ne**
nam, *conj.,* for
namque, *conj.,* for, for in fact
nanciscor, -ī, nanctus sum, to come across, meet, acquire, arrive at
narrō (1), to relate, tell, narrate
nascor, -ī, nātus sum, to be born
Nausistrata, -ae, *m.,* a Greek name
nāvis, -is, *f.,* a ship
nē, *affirmative particle,* yes, truly
nē, *negative adv. and conj.,* not, that not, lest
-ne, *interr. particle that marks sentence as a question*
ne . . . quidem, *adv.,* not even
nec, *conj.,* and not, nor
necesse, *n. indecl.,* necessary, inevitable
necopīnans, -ntis, *adj.,* not expecting, unaware
neglegentia, -ae, *f.,* carelessness, negligence
negō (1), to deny
negōtium, -ī, *n.,* business, occupation
nēmō, -inis, *m.,* no one
nempe, *particle,* truly, certainly, to be sure

Neptūnus, -ī, *m.,* Neptune
neque, *conj.,* and not, nor
nequeō, -īre, -īvī/-iī, —, to not be able to
nēquis, -qua/-quae, -quid, *indef. pron.,* no one, nothing
nēquō, *adv.,* to no place, nowhere
nesciō, -īre, -īvī/-iī, -ītum, to not know, be ignorant of
nescīōquis, -quid, *indef. pron.,* someone, something
nēve, *conj.,* nor
Nīcēratus, -ī, *m.,* a Greek name
nihil, *n. indecl.,* nothing
nīl, *n. indecl.,* nothing
nimis, *adv.,* very much, too much, excessively
nimium, *adv.,* very much, too much, excessively
nisi, *conj.,* unless, if not
nōbilis, -is, -e, *adj.,* well-known, noble, impressively grand
nōlō, nōlle, nōluī, —, to not want to, to be unwilling
nōmen, -inis, *n.,* a name
nōn, *adv.,* no, not
nōnnumquam, *adv.,* sometimes
nōs, nostrī/nostrum, *pers. pron.,* we, us
noscō, -ere, nōvī, nōtum, to get to know, learn
noster, -tra, -trum, *adj.,* our
novīcius, -a, -um, *adj.,* new, newly enslaved
novus, -a, -um, *adj.,* new, young, strange
nox, -ctis, *f.,* a night, nighttime

noxius, -a, -um, *adj.,* harmful, guilty

nullus, -a, -um, *adj.,* none, no

num, *interr. particle that expects a negative answer*

numquam, *adv.,* never

numquis, numquid, *interr. pron.,* who? what? (in a question expecting a negative answer)

nunc, *adv.,* now

nunciam, *adv.,* right now, this very instant

nuntiō (1), to announce

nuntius, -ī, *m.,* a messenger

nuptiae, -ārum, *f. pl.,* a marriage, wedding

nurus, -ūs, *f.,* a daughter-in-law

nusquam, *adv.,* nowhere

ō, *interj.,* oh (can express admiration, pleasure, horror, etc.; also used for addressing someone)

ob, *prep.* + *acc.,* in front of, in return for, because of

obdō, -ere, -didī, -ditum, to put before or against, to bolt the door

obiciō, -ere, -iēcī, -iectum, to throw in the way, expose, put before, bring up

obsecrō (1), to beg, implore, ask

obsequium, -ī, *n.,* compliance, indulgence, submission

obsequor, -ī, -cūtus sum, to comply with, give in to, obey

observō (1), to watch, observe

obstō, -āre, -itī, -ātum, to stand before or against, to oppose, hinder

obtundō, -ere, -udī, -ūsum/ -unsum, to beat, thump, make dull

obviam, *adv.,* in the way, on the way

occāsiō, -ōnis, *f.,* an opportunity, occasion

occipiō, -ere, -cēpī, -ceptum, to begin

ōcius, *compar. adv.,* quicker, quite quickly

oculus, -ī, *m.,* an eye

ōdī, ōdisse, ōsum, *defective verb,* to hate, detest

odiōsus, -a, -um, *adj.,* hateful, troublesome

odium, -ī, *n.,* hatred

officium, -ī, *n.,* a duty

ōh, *interj.,* oh (an expression of various emotions: pleasure, pain, surprise, etc.)

ōlim, *adv.,* once, for a long time, formerly, in the future

omissior, -ior, -ius, *compar. adj.,* more or quite negligent, remiss

omittō, -ere, -mīsī, -missum, to let go, give up, leave out

omnīnō, *adv.,* entirely, altogether

omnis, -is, -e, *adj.,* each, every, all

opera, -ae, *f.,* trouble, labor, work

opīniō, -ōnis, *f.,* opinion, reputation, rumor

opīnor, -ārī, -ātus sum, to
believe, suppose, guess

oportet, -ēre, -uit, —, impers.,
it is proper, one ought

oppidō, adv., quite, very much,
certainly

opportūnē, adv., suitably,
conveniently

opprimō, -ere, -pressī,
-pressum, to press upon,
catch, surprise

optātus, -a, -um, adj., desired,
welcome

optineō, -ēre, -tinuī, -tentum,
to hold, take hold of,
maintain

optō (1), to choose, select, wish

optumē, adv., best, excellent

opus, -eris, n., work, labor; +
abl., there is need of.

ōrātiō, -ōnis, f., speaking, a
speech

orior, -īrī, -tus sum, to arise,
rise

ornō (1), to prepare, equip,
furnish, adorn

ōs, ōris, n., the mouth, face

ostendō, -ere, -dī, -sum/-tum,
to show, display

ostentō (1), to hold out, present,
offer, show

ostium, -ī, n., a door

ōtium, -ī, n., free time, leisure,
peace

pactum, -ī, n., an agreement,
arrangement

Pamphīlus, -ī, m., a Greek
name

pār, paris, adj., equal, like,
appropriate

parasītus, -ī, m., a dinner guest,
parasite

parātus, -a, -um, adj., prepared,
ready, provided

parcē, adv., sparingly, frugally

parcō, parcere, pepercī, —, to
spare, be sparing, frugal

parcus, -a, -um, adj., sparing,
frugal

parens, -ntis, m./f., a parent

pariō, parere, peperī, partum,
to give birth, produce, create

Parmenō, -ōnis, m., a Greek
name

parō (1), to prepare, make
ready, provide, furnish

pars, -tis, f., part, portion, role,
direction

parvolus, -a, -um, adj., very
small, very little

parvos, -a, -om, adj., small,
little

pater, -tris, m., a father

patior, -ī, passus sum, to
endure, bear

patria, -ae, f., homeland

patrius, -a, -um, adj., relating
or belonging to the father

patrocinor, -ārī, -ātus sum, to
protect, defend

patruos, -ī, m., a paternal uncle

paucus, -a, -um, adj., few

paullō, adv., by a little

paupertās, -ātis, f., humble
circumstances

peccātum, -ī, n., a fault,
mistake, sin

peccō (1), to make a mistake, sin

pedisequa, -ae, *f.,* an attendant, waiting-woman

pēior, -ior, -ius, *compar. adj.,* worse

pellō, -ere, pepulī, pulsum, to strike, knock, push, drive away

pendō, -ere, pependī, pensum, to hang, weigh, consider, value

per, *prep.* + *acc.,* through, because of

percutiō, -ere, -cussī, -cussum, to strike, strike through, pierce

perdō, -ere, -didī, -ditum, to destroy, ruin, waste, lose

perdūcō, -ere, -xī, -ctum, to lead through, bring along or to

perdūrō (1), to last a long time, endure

peregrē, *adv.,* in a foreign country, abroad

pereō, -īre, -īvī/-iī, -itum, to go through, perish, be ruined

perferō, perferre, pertulī, perlātum, to carry through, bear to the end, bring to an end

pergō, -ere, perrexī, perrectum, to continue, proceed

perīclum, -ī, *n.,* an attempt, trial, danger

perinde, *adv.,* in a like manner, just as if

perlongē, *adv.,* very far

pernoscō, -ere, -nōvī, -nōtum, to get to know thoroughly, learn thoroughly

perpetior, -ī, -pessus sum, to endure or bear to the end

perpetuos, -a, -om, *adj.,* continuous, uninterrupted

persolvō, -ere, -vī, -ūtum, to unloose, explain, pay off

perstrepō, -ere, —, —, to make a loud noise

pertinācia, -ae, *f.,* firmness, stubbornness

perturbō (1), to disturb thoroughly, upset, alarm

pessulus, -ī, *m.,* a bolt

Phaedria, -ae, *m.,* a Greek name

Phaedrus, -ī, *m.,* a Greek name

Phīdippus, -ī, *m.,* a Greek name

philosophus, -ī, *m.,* a philosopher

Philūmenā, -ae, *f.,* a Greek name

Phormiō, -ōnis, *m.,* a Greek name

pictūra, -ae, *f.,* a painting

pictus, -a, -um, *adj.,* painted

Pīraeus, -ī, *m.,* the port of Athens

plācābilius, *compar. adv.,* more or quite appeasing or easy to appease

placeō, -ēre, -uī, -itum, to be pleasing, be acceptable

placidus, -a, -um, *adj.,* quiet, still, gentle

plācō (1), to soothe, calm, appease, reconcile

Plautus, -ī, *m.,* a Roman name
plēnus, -a, -um, *adj.,* full
plērusque, -aque, -umque, *adj.,* very many, a large part, the most part
plūrumum, *adv.,* most
plūs, *adv.,* more
plūs, -ris, *n.,* more
poēta, -ae, *m.,* a poet
pol, *interj.,* by Pollux!
pollen, -inis, *n.,* fine flour, meal
polliceor, -ērī, -itus sum, to make an offer, promise
populus, -ī, *m.,* people, a crowd, the community
porrō, *adv.,* forward, further, in the future, again, next
portō (1), to carry, bring
possideō, -ēre, -ēdi, -essum, to possess, have, hold
possum, posse, potuī, —, to be able to
post, *adv.,* behind, after
posterior, -ior, -ius, *compar. adj.,* following after, next, later
posthabeō, -ēre, -uī, -itum, to value less, treat as less important
postquam, *conj.,* after, when
postulō (1), to demand
Postumius, -ī, *m.,* a Roman name
potens, -ntis, *adj.,* able, powerful
potestās, -ātis, *f.,* power, authority, ability
potior, -īrī, -ītus sum, to get possession of, to possess, to be master of
potius, *adv.,* rather

pōtō (1), to drink
praebeō, -ēre, -uī, -itum, to offer, hold out, provide
praedicō (1), to declare, proclaim
praedīcō, -ere, -xī, -ctum, to say beforehand, predict, instruct
praeditus, -a, -um, *adj.,* endowed with, provided with
praeficiō, -ere, -fēcī, -fectum, to put in charge
Praenestīnus, -ī, *m.,* a Roman name
praepōnō, -ere, -posuī, -positum, to put before, put in charge, prefer
praesagiō, -īre, -īvī, —, to presage, have a presentiment of
praesens, -ntis, *adj.,* present, immediate, effective, favorable
praeter, *prep. + acc.,* beyond, except, besides
praetereō, -īre, -īvī/-iī, -itum, to pass, pass by, pass over
prāvus, -a, -om, *adj.,* crooked, irregular, depraved
pretium, -ī, *n.,* worth, value, price
prex, precis, *f.,* a request, entreaty, prayer
prīdem, *adv.,* long ago, long since
prīmārius, -a, -um, *adj.,* in the first rank, distinguished
prīmō, *adv.,* at first
prīmus, -a, -um, *adj.,* first, foremost

principiō, *adv.,* first of all, to start with

principium, -ī, *n.,* the beginning

prius, *adv.,* before, previously

prius . . . quam, *conj.,* before

prō, *prep.* + *abl.,* in front of, in place of, on behalf of, for, in reward for

prō, *interj.,* oh!, ah! (an expression of wonder, disapproval, or grief)

probē, *adv.,* well, rightly, properly, excellently

procax, -ācis, *adj.,* shameless, bold

prōcēdō, -ere, -cessī, -cessum, to go ahead, proceed, come out

prōclīve, -is, *adj.,* inclined towards, prone

procul, *adv.,* far, far way, at a distance

prōcūrō (1), to take care of, look after

prōdeō, -īre, -iī, -itum, to go ahead, come out, appear

profectō, *adv.,* really, truly, indeed

prōferō, prōferre, prōtulī, prōlātum, to bring forward, make known

prohibeō, -ēre, -uī, -itum, to hold back, restrain, forbid

proin, *see* **proinde**

proinde, *adv.,* consequently, then, just as if

properō (1), to hasten, hurry, be quick

propter, *prep.* + *acc.,* on account of, because of

proptereā, *adv.,* on that account, therefore

prorsum, *adv.,* straight-forward

prōruō, -ere, -ruī, -rutum, to rush forward

prosperē, *adv.,* prosperously, fortunately, favorably

prospiciō, -ere, -spexī, -spectum, to look out, look ahead

prōvocō (1), to call out, provoke.

proxumus, -a, -um, *superl. adj.,* nearest, closest, readiest

psaltria, -ae, *f.,* a female player on, or singer to, the cithara

pūblicitus, *adv.,* at public expense, publicly

pudet, -ēre, -uit/-itum est, *impers.,* to cause shame, to shame

pudīcē, *adv.,* modestly, chastely.

puella, -ae, *f.,* a girl.

puer, -erī, *m.,* a boy

puerīlis, -is, -e, *adj.,* youthful, childish

pueritia, -ae, *f.,* childhood

pugnō (1), to fight, struggle

pugnus, -ī, *m.,* the fist

purgō (1), to cleanse, defend, justify

putō (1), to reckon, consider, think

quaeritō (1), to seek out eagerly, ask eagerly about

quaerō, -ere, quaesīvī/quaesiī, quaesītum, to seek for, inquire into, demand

quaesō, (-ere), —, —, to look for, beg, ask

quaestus, -ūs, *m.,* profit, gain, advantage, an occupation

quam, *interr. and rel. adv.,* how, in what way

quandō, *indef., interr., and rel. adv.,* when, since

quantus, -a, -um, *interr. and rel. adj.,* how much, how great, of what size

quāpropter, *interr. and rel. adv.,* why, for what reason

quasi, *adv.,* as if, just as

-que, *conj.,* and

queror, -ī, -stus sum, to complain, lament

quī, quae, quod, *indef., interr., and rel. adj. and pron.,* who, which, what

quia, *conj.,* since, because

quīdam, quaedam, quoddam, *adj.,* a certain one

quidem, *particle,* really, truly, indeed, even

quīn, *adv.,* why not?, no, rather; *conj.,* who not, that not, but that

quis, quid, *interr. and rel. pron. and adj.,* who, which, what

quisnam, quaenam, quidnam, *interr. pron. and adj.,* who, which, what

quisquam, quicquam, *indef. pron.,* anyone, anything

quisque, quaeque, quidque, *adj. and pron.,* each, each one

quisquis, quidquid, *pron. and adj.,* whoever, whatever

quīvīs, quaevīs, quodvīs, *adj.,* anyone or anything at all

quō, *adv.,* to where, to what place

quod, *conj.,* the fact that, as to the fact that, because

quom, *rel. adv.,* when, since, although

quomque, *adv.,* at any time

quondam, *adv.,* at one time, once, formerly

quoque, *adv.,* also, too

quōr, *interr. adv.,* why, for what reason

quorsum, *rel. adv.,* to what place, for what purpose

rapiō, -ere, -uī, -tum, to snatch, seize, tear away

ratiō, -ōnis, *f.,* reason, reasoning, reckoning, consideration

recipiō, -ere, -cēpī, -ceptum, to take back, receive

rectē, *adv.,* rightly, properly, well

rectius, *adv.,* more or quite rightly, properly, well

reddō, -ere, -idī, -itum, to return, give back, restore, deliver

reddūcō, -ere, -xī, -ctum, to lead or bring back, bring home

redeō, redīre, rediī, reditum, to go or come back, return

redigō, -ere, redēgī, redactum, to drive back, bring back

refellō, -ere, -ī, —, to refute, disprove

rēfert, rēferre, rētulit, —, it concerns, it matters

rēiciō, -ere, -iēcī, -iectum, to throw back

relicuos, -a, -om, *adj.,* left behind, remaining; *n.,* what remains, the future

religiō, -ōnis, *f.,* religious awe, a prohibition

relinquō, -ere, -līquī, -lictum, to leave, leave behind

remittō, -ere, -mīsī, -missum, to send back, let go, relax, yield

reor, rērī, ratus sum, to reckon, think, judge, suppose

reperiō, -īre, repperī, repertum, to find, find out, discover

reprehendō, -ere, -dī, -sum, to catch again, seize, restrain, blame, reproach

reprimō, -ere, -pressī, -pressum, to hold back, restrain, hinder

repudiō (1), to refuse, reject, disdain

repudium, -ī, *n.,* a divorce, the breaking of an engagement

reputō (1), to think over, reconsider, calculate out

rēs, reī, *f.,* a thing, matter, affair, property, possessions, interest, advantage, case, cause

rescīscō, -ere, -scīvī/-sciī, -scītum, to find out, ascertain

rescrībō, -ere, -psī, -ptum, to write again, write back, to pay back in writing (by having it transferred to the creditor's account)

respīrō (1), to breathe again, recover one's breath, take a breath

respondeō, -ēre, -sī, -sum, to answer, reply, correspond to

restringuō, -ere, -nxī, -nctum, to bind back or tight, draw back, restrain

retineō, -ēre, -tinuī, -tentum, to hold back, restrain, keep, maintain

revortor, -ī, -sus sum, to turn back, come back, return

rīdiculus, -a, -um, *adj.,* humorous, funny, absurd

rogitō (1), to ask frequently or eagerly

rogō (1), to ask, inquire, question

rūmor, -ōris, *m.,* rumor, general opinion

rursum, *adv.,* backwards, back, again

rūs, rūris, *n.,* the country

saepe, *adv.,* often

saevus, -a, -om, *adj.,* savage, fierce, cruel

salvē, salvēte, *defective verb,* be well, greetings, farewell

salvos, -a, -om, *adj.,* safe, sound, well

sanctē, *adv.,* solemnly, religiously, virtuously

sānē, *adv.,* really, surely, to be sure

sānus, -a, -um, *adj.,* sound, healthy, sane

sapienter, *adv.,* wisely

sapiō, -ere, -īvī/-iī, —, to taste, have good taste, be sensible, be wise

sat, *see* **satis**

satagō, -ere, -ēgī, -actum, to bustle about, fuss over, busy oneself with

satis, *adv.,* enough

satius, *compar. adv.,* better, more advantageous

scelus, -eris, *n.,* a crime, evil deed, misfortune

scīlicet, *particle,* evidently, certainly, of course

sciō, -īre, -īvī/-iī, -ītum, to know, know how to, understand

sciscitor, -ārī, -ātus sum, to inquire thoroughly, examine, ask

scītus, -a, -um, *adj.,* knowing, sensible, pretty

scortor, -ārī, —, to go whoring

scrībō, -ere, -psī, -ptum, to write

scriptūra, -ae, *f.,* a piece of writing, composition

scrūpulus, -ī, *m.,* a small stone, worry, anxiety, scruple

sē, *reflex. pron.,* himself, herself, itself

secundus, -a, -um, *adj.,* following, favorable, second

secus, *adv.,* otherwise, otherwise than

sed, *conj.,* but

sedeō, -ēre, sēdī, sessum, to sit

semel, *adv.,* once, for the first time, first

semper, *adv.,* always

senectūs, -ūtis, *f.,* old age

senex, -is, *m.,* an old man

sententia, -ae, *f.,* an opinion, thought, purpose

sentiō, -īre, -sī, -sum, to perceive, think, feel

sepeliō, -īre, -elīvī/-eliī, -ultum, to bury, put an end to, ruin

sepulcrum, -ī, *n.,* a place of burial, grave, tomb

sequor, -ī, -cūtus sum, to follow, accompany, attend

sermō, -ōnis, *m.,* talk, conversation

serviō, -īre, -īvī/-iī, -ītum, to be a slave to

servitūs, -ūtis, *f.,* slavery

servō (1), to watch over, keep, preserve, save

servolus, -ī, *m.,* a little slave

servos, -ī, *m.,* a male slave

sēsē, *see* **sē**

sī, *conj.,* if

sīc, *adv.,* so, thus, in this way, like this

signum, -ī, *n.,* a sign, mark, token

similis, -is, -e, *adj.,* like, similar

Simō, -ōnis, *m.,* a Greek name

simul, *adv.,* at the same time, together

simulō (1), to pretend, put on the appearance

sīn, *conj.,* but if (on the other hand)

sine, *prep. + abl.,* without

sinō,-ere, sīvī/siī, situm, to put down, leave alone, permit, allow

sīquis, sīquid, *pron.,* if anyone, if anything

situs, -a, -um, *adj.,* placed, lying, situated

socrus, -ūs, *f.,* a mother-in-law

sōdēs, *contraction of sī audēs,* please, if you please

soleō, -ēre, —, -itum, to be accustomed to

sollicitō (1), to disturb, shake, trouble

sollicitūdō, -inis, *f.,* uneasiness, anxiety, disquiet

sōlus, -a, -um, *adj.,* alone, only, sole

solvō, -ere, -ī, -ūtum, to loosen, free

somnus, -ī, *m.,* sleep

sonitus, -ūs, *m.,* a sound, noise

soror, -ōris, *f.,* a sister

Sōsia, -ae, *m.,* a Greek name

Sōstrata, -ae, *f.,* a Greek name

spatium, -ī, *n.,* a span, a space (in distance or time)

spectātor, -ōris, *m.,* a watcher, observer, spectator

spectātus, -a, -um, *adj.,* tested, approved

spectō (1), to look at carefully, observe, contemplate

spēs, speī, *f.,* hope, expectation

status, -ūs, *m.,* standing, position, state, condition

stimulō (1), to goad, prick, incite, annoy

stipula, -ae, *f.,* a stalk

stō, stāre, stetī, statum, to stand

studeō, -ēre, -uī, —, to be eager for, strive after, be busy with

studium, -ī, *n.,* an inclination, eagerness, interest, pursuit

stultē, *adv.,* stupidly, foolishly

sub, *prep.* + *abl.,* under, beneath

subdūcō, -ere, -xī, -ctum, to draw up from under, raise, remove, steal, take account of

submoveō, -ēre, -mōvī, -mōtum, to move up from below, move away, drive off, remove

subvortō, -ere, -vortī, -vorsum, to overturn, overthrow, ruin

succurrō, -ere, -currī, -cursum, to run up under, come to mind, run to the aid of

sum, esse, fuī, —, to be

summus, -a, -um, *adj.,* the highest, largest, greatest, the sum total

sūmō, -ere, sumpsī, sumptum, to take up, use, spend

sumptuōsus, -a, -um, *adj.,* costly, expensive, lavish, extravagant

sumptus, -ūs, *m.,* cost, expense

suus, -a, -um, *adj.,* his own, her own, its own

superbē, *adv.,* proudly, arrogantly

superbia, -ae, *f.,* pride, arrogance

supplex, -icis, *adj.,* kneeling, supplicating; *m./f.* a suppliant

suprā, *adv.,* to a higher degree, more, over

surdus, -a, -um, *adj.,* deaf

suscipiō, -ere, -cēpī, -ceptum, to take up, receive

suspectō (1), to keep looking at

suspicor, -ārī, -ātus sum, to suspect, suppose

symbola, -ae, *f.,* a contribution of money to a common feast

Synapothnēscontes, -ōn, *proper noun,* the name of a play, Greek for *Those Who Die Together*

Syrus, -ī, *m.,* a Greek name

tabula, -ae, *f.,* a board, tablet, painting

taceō, -ēre, -uī, -itum, to be silent, quiet, to say nothing

tacitus, -a, -um, *adj.,* silent, quiet

tacturnitās, -ātis, *f.,* silence, quiet

tālis, -is, -e, *adj.,* of such a kind, such

tam, *adv.,* so, so far, to such a degree

tamen, *adv.,* never the less

tandem, *adv.,* finally, after all, at last

tantō opere, *adv.,* so greatly, so much

tantus, -a, -um, *adj.,* so much, so great, of such a size

tantusdem, -adem, -undem, *adj.,* just as much, just as great, of just the same size

tēgula, -ae, *f.,* a roof-tile

tēla, -ae, *f.,* weaving, a loom

templum, -ī, *n.,* a section, region, a temple

tempus, -oris, *n.,* a time, an opportunity

tenax, -ācis, *adj.,* grasping, clinging

teneō, -ēre, -uī, -tum, to have, hold, to remember (i.e. have in one's memory)

Terentius, -ī, *m.,* a Roman name

terra, -ae, *f.,* earth, ground, land

Thāis, -idis, *f.,* a Greek name

tībia, -ae, *f.,* a pipe, flute.

timeō, -ēre, uī, —, to fear, be afraid

tolerābilis, -is, -e, *adj.,* tolerable, bearable; tolerant, patient

tolerō (1), to carry, endure, bear, maintain, keep up

tōtus, -a, -um, *adj.,* the whole, complete, entire

trādō, -ere, -didī, -ditum, to hand over, give up

transeō, -īre, -īvī/-iī, -itum, to go over

triennium, -ī, *n.,* a period of three years

trīgintā, *indecl. adj.,* thirty

tristis, -is, -e, *adj.,* sad, gloomy

truculentus, -a, -um, *adj.,* rough, savage, cruel

tū, tuī, *pers. pron.,* you (*sn.*)

tum, *adv.,* then, at that time

tuos, -a, -om, *adj.,* your

turba, -ae, *f.,* a tumult, disturbance, crowd

Turpiō, -ōnis, *m.,* a Roman name

turpis, -is, -e, *adj.,* ugly,
disgraceful, shameful
tūte, *see* **tū**
tūtus, -a, -um, *adj.,* safe,
watchful

ubi, *interr., rel., and indef. adv.,*
where, when
ubinam, *interr. adv.,* where, just
where
ulciscor, -ī, -cultus sum, to take
vengeance, punish
ullus, -a, -um, *adj.,* any
ultrō, *adv.,* beyond, of one's
own accord
umquam, *adv.,* at any time, ever
ūnā, *adv.,* together with
unde, *interr. and rel. adv.,* from
where
ūnicē, *adv.,* singly, especially,
particularly
ūnicus, -a, -um, *adj.,* only, sole,
singular
ūnivorsus, -a, -um, *adj.,* whole,
entire, all together
ūnus, -a, -um, *adj.,* one
urbs, -bis, *f.,* a city
usque, *adv.,* at all times,
continuously, up until
ūsus, -ūs, *m.,* use, practice,
opportunity
ut, *adv. and conj.,* how, just as,
when, so that, in order that
utī, *see* **ut**
ūtilis, -is, -e, *adj.,* useful, fit,
beneficial
ūtor, ūtī, ūsus sum, to use,
make use of, enjoy, find
uxor, -ōris, *f.,* a wife

vae, *interj.,* oh! (an expression
of anguish)
vāh, *interj.,* oh, ah (an
expression of various
emotions: surprise, pain,
understanding, etc.)
valeō, -ēre, -uī, -ītum, to be
strong, farewell
Valerius, -ī, *m.,* a Roman name
vehemens, -ntis, *adj.,*
vehement, furious,
impetuous
vel, *particle,* either, or, even
veniō, -īre, vēnī, ventum, to
come
vēnor, -ārī, -ātus sum, to hunt,
go hunting
venter, -tris, *m.,* the belly,
stomach
ventulus, -ī, *m.,* a slight wind,
gentle breeze
venustus, -a, -um, *adj.,*
charming, lovely, graceful
verbum, -ī, *n.,* a word, saying
vērē, *adv.,* truly, really, rightly
vereor, -ērī, -itus sum, to fear,
revere
vēritās, -atis, *f.,* truth
vērō, *adv. and particle,* in truth,
really, indeed
vērum, *conj.,* but, never the less,
still
vērus, -a, -um, *adj.,* true
vesperascō, -ere, -āvī, —, to
become evening
vestiō, -īre, -īvī/-iī, -ītum, to
dress, clothe
vestis, -is, *f.,* a garment,
clothing

vestītus, -ūs, *m.,* clothes,
clothing, attire
vetus, -eris, *adj.,* old
via, -ae, *f.,* a path, road
vīcīnia, -ae, *f.,* a neighborhood
vīcīnus, -a, -um, *adj.,*
neighboring; *m./f.,* a
neighbor
victus, -ūs, *m.,* a living,
sustenance, way of life
videō, -ēre, vīdī, vīsum, to see
vincō, -ere, vīcī, victum, to
conquer, defeat
vir, virī, *m.,* a man, husband
virgō, -inis, *f.,* an young girl,
unmarried girl
virīlis, -is, -e, *adj.,* manly
virtūs, -ūtis, *f.,* excellence,
virtue, courage

vīs, vis, *f.,* force, power, violence
vīsō, -ere, -ī, —, to look at
closely, go to see, visit
vīta, -ae, *f.,* life, way of life
vitium, -ī, *n.,* a fault, mistake, sin
vīvō, -ere, vixī, victum, to live,
be alive
vix, *adv.,* scarcely, barely, hardly
volō, velle, voluī, —, to want,
wish, be willing
voltus, -ūs, *m.,* face, expression,
look
voluptās, -ātis, *f.,* pleasure,
delight
vōs, vostrum/vostrī, *pers. pron,*
you (*pl.*)
voster, -tra, -trum, *adj.,* your
vox, vōcis, *f.,* voice, call,
utterance